BLACK CLASSICAL MUSICIANS OF THE TWENTIETH CENTURY

Volume I

By

E. Harrison Gordon

SECOND EDITION

**BLACK CLASSICAL MUSICIANS
OF THE TWENTIETH CENTURY**

Volume I

By

E. Harrison Gordon

SECOND EDITION

Copyright, E. Harrison Gordon, August 1973
Revisions for Publishing completed July 1977
Second Edition August 2016

Library of Congress Cataloging in Publication Data

      Gordon, E. Harrison.
          Black classical musicians of the twentieth century.

          Bibliography: p.
          Includes Index.
          1.   Afro-American musicians—Biography. I.
      Title.

      ISBN 978-0-692-76843-3

AUTHOR'S BIOGRAPHY

Mr. Gordon is a mature native of New York. He received his B.A. from Brooklyn College, where he majored in music. He has an M.A. in Music Education from Teachers College, Columbia University, where he majored in conducting and minored in voila.

He was a vocal music teacher for the Department of Education and served in that capacity from 1972 to 2014. At the time of the first edition he was the conductor of the Brandeis High School Chorus. He organized the Gordon Chorale in 1966. During its existence Mr. Gordon was also the conductor for the Chorale from 1966 to 1986. Since its inception the Chorale has made three radio appearances and one cable television appearance. The Chorale has also performed on several college campuses and received press coverage in the New York Times, The Daily news and The Amsterdam news. This organization has produced one record, which included Schubert's "Mass in G", various excerpts from the standard repertoire and Afro-American Spirituals. Also, the Gordon Chorale released a recording of Afro-American Spirituals for the Musical Heritage Society.

This book is Mr. Gordon's first independent publication.

PREFACE

I would like to avail myself of this opportunity to thank the staff of the Schomburg Collection for their indispensible cooperation during the initial research period. I would like also like to thank all of the artists and their relatives for their cooperation.

When Dr. Hall Johnson died it became all too clear to me that another one of our great Black Classical Musicians had died and that there were few if any books written about him that mentioned his works and the main events of his life. I became determined at that point to make a record of the Classical Musicians of Dr. Johnson's generation for the young Blacks of my generation. It became obvious that now would be the perfect time to document the lives of some of our contemporary black Classical artists as well and I have included some of these musicians also.

I began to realize that there were people like Roland Hayes who had passed through most of their career and began to go into semi-retirement before I was old enough to understand their work. I knew then that a record of these people's accomplishments had to be brought to the attention of my contemporaries lest by some trick of fate most of them should leave this world without ever having known this side of their heritage. With these thoughts running through my mind I sat down and began to research and write.

During the course of my research I found that Maude Cuney-Hare had had a similar idea and publish a book of this type in 1936 and although her book is still well worth reading a lot has happened between 1936 and 1970.

The research began to mushroom because the study of the life of one Black Musician would reveal the name of another and it kept on going. I finally had to put an end to this by pulling together those musicians whose research I had completed, in this volume and laying aside the others until such time as I would be free to prepare the next volume. I have used the terms "Black" and Afro-American" as much as possible because these are the terms that my people want now. But I do not wish for my people to become overly concerned with the term "Black" instead of being concerned with what it means to think, act, accomplish and most of all "*research*" Black.

4

Some of the people in this book felt at home with the term "Negro" but they were no less Black than you or I. They proved this by their actions. Most of all, they proved that it is not so much what you call yourself as what you, "*Think of yourself*" and "*Do with yourself.*" "*As a man thinketh so is he.*"

I have tried to be as accurate as possible. With only two exceptions, all of the information in this book has been verified by either the artist, a member of his or her staff or the next of kin.

The time has come to make as many documents about our heritage as possible.

E. Harrison Gordon

CREDITS

American Society of Composers, Authors and Publishers (ASCAP)
Belwin Mills Publishing Company
Columbia Record Company
Mrs. Alice J. Foster (sister of Dr. Hall Johnson)
Galaxy Music Company
Harvard University
Miss Afrika Hayes (daughter of Roland Hayes)
Mrs. James Weldon Johnson
Metropolitan Opera Archives
Mr. Paul Robeson Jr.
Rutgers University
Dr. Georgia A. Ryder (Mrs. Noah Francis Ryder)
Schomburg Collection (New York Public Library at 135th St. , N.Y.C.)
Summy Birchard Publishing Company
Vanguard Record Company
Ms. Alex Williamson (Manager to Mr. Andre Watts)
Mrs. Edith McFall Work (Mrs. John W. Work III)

Also, I would like to thank Kim Kirkley of WriteitWisely.com for her immense contributions to the publishing of this second edition.

TABLE OF CONTENTS

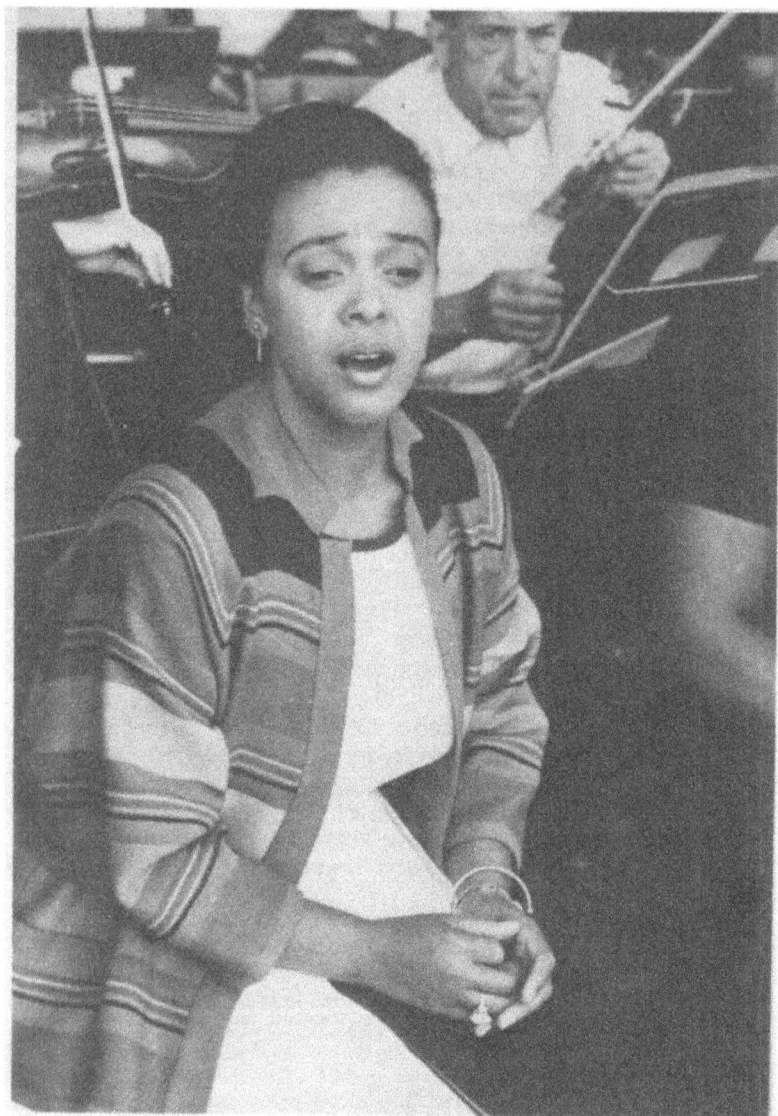

Adele Addison
Picture Courtesy New York Public Library, Lincoln Center
Fred Fehl Photographer

Adele Addison
July 24, 1925
Soprano, Teacher

Adele Addison was born in Springfield, Massachusetts. Her parent's names were Julius B. Addison and Janette Taylor Addison. Miss Addison was raised by her aunt and uncle in Springfield. She received some of her vocal training from Madam Ruth Eckberg. She attended Springfield High School. In 1946, Miss Addison completed her Bachelor of Music degree at Westminster Choir College in Princeton, New Jersey.

During her adolescent years she did various jobs to support herself, including working in an armory, running an elevator in a department store and working in a hospital.

Miss Addison made her concert debut at Jordan Hall in Boston, Massachusetts. During the 1945 and 1956 season she appeared both with the Springfield and the Greenfield Symphony Orchestras. Later that season she sang in a performance of "The Redemption" by Gounod in her hometown.

In 1946 she appeared as a soloist with the Boston Symphony orchestra in a performance of "The Martyrdom of St. Sebastian" by Debussy. This performance was conducted by Charles Munch.

Among other notable engagements, she has appeared at Tanglewood in the Berkshire Festival and the New England Opera Theater. In 1947 she was runner up in the Paul Lavalle award contest conducted by the National Federation of Music Clubs. In 1955 she made her Operatic Debut with the New York City Opera Company. In 1957 she was one of the representatives of the New York City Opera Company who received the proclamation from Mayor Wagner declaring the week of November 1st as "New York City Opera Week." The New York City Opera Company celebrated its 15th anniversary that year. It is a pity that we no longer observe this week. In 1958 she did another performance at the Berkshire Music Festival. This time she appeared with the Boston Symphony Orchestra in a performance of Beethoven's "Ninth Symphony." She performed the World Premiere of the "Gloria" by Poulenc with the Boston Symphony Orchestra under the direction of Charles Munch.

Later in 1958 she married Norman Berger, who was a research scientist and clinical professor of prosthetics and orthotics at New York University. After 47 years of marriage, they were parted by his death in 2005.

During the early 1960's, Miss Addison was awarded an Honorary Doctorate from the University of Massachusetts. In 1962 she appeared with Madame Rosina Lhévinne and the Juilliard Quartet at Carnegie Hall. In 1963 Miss Addison performed in 5 major Russian Cities including Moscow, on a tour arranged by Sol Hurok. She has also studied at New England Conservatory, the Juilliard School of Music, Povla Frijsh and performed at the Metropolitan Museum of Art.

Miss Addison has served as soloist of the Fifth Avenue Presbyterian Church of New York City.

Retired now, she was a member of the faculty at the New York State University at Stony Brook, Eastman School of Music, the Aspen Music School and the Manhattan School of Music for many years. To add to her many honors, in 2001 she received an honorary doctorate from the Manhattan School of Music.

Her recordings include:
(Columbia)   "The Messiah" by Handel (with the New York Philharmonic under Leonard Bernstein)

"   "Ode for St. Cecilia" by Handel (New York Philharmonic under Bernstein)

"   "Martyrdom of St. Sebastian" by Debussy (N.Y. Philharmonic - Bernstein)

"   "Time Cycle" by Lucas Foss (World Premiere) N.Y> Philharmonic - Bernstein)

"   "Porgy and Bess" by Gershwin

"   "Israel in Egypt" by Handel

She has also recorded some contemporary chamber music.

10

Sanford Allen

Sanford Allen
February 26, 1939-
Violinist

Early in July of 1976 while drawing up the final draft of this book, I had the good fortune to have an interview with Sanford Allen. The following sketch is a result of that interview.

Sanford Allen was born in New York City. To be a little more specific he was born in Harlem. His family moved to Bedford-Stuyvesant when he was two years old and that is where he grew up. His father, Willis E. Allen was a photographer, born in Harris, Kentucky and his mother, Allene L. Allen, was born in Boulder, Colorado. She is a trained school teacher, who worked as a teacher's aide because of the seniority situation with the Board of Education. Mr. Allen has one brother, Frederick and one sister, Anita.

Sanford Allen is married and his wife's professional name is Madhur Jaffrey. A lecturer, writer, cookbook author and actress, she is from India and teaches cooking at the James Beard School, a private cooking school. The Allens have three daughters: Zia , Meera and Sakina. One of their daughters is studying voice.

At five years of age Sanford Allen began to study piano with his mother and he continued to do so until age seven. At age seven he began to study the violin. When he was 10 he entered the Juilliard School Music as a scholarship student. While at Juilliard he studied violin with Madame Vera Fonaroff.

While he was growing up he sometimes felt "disconnected." He said that there were not a great many Blacks studying classical music and there was always the realization that he was not white. Mr. Allen attended the High School of Performing Arts.

In 1956 at the age of 17 he won the Federation of Music Clubs Award at the Berkshire Music Festival. He worked on his Bachelors of Music for almost fours years at the Mannes College of Music. He continued his studies with Madame Fonaroff at Mannes.

12

In his senior year at Mannes came the opportunity of a lifetime: A chance to play in New York Philharmonic. Mr. Allen stated that this was a very difficult decision to make. He was very close to completing his Bachelor of Music degree when this opportunity came. Torn between staying in school and seizing the chance to play in an established, prestigious orchestra, he decided to join the New York Philharmonic. Thus in 1959 at the age of 20 he became one of the youngest musicians to join the Lewisohn Stadium Orchestra since its inception. (This was at one time a summer orchestra composed primarily of members of the New York Philharmonic.) In 1961 he was again asked to play in the Lewisohn Stadium Orchestra. Finally in 1962 he became a regular member of the New York Philharmonic Orchestra, and became the first Black to ever be hired by the New York Philharmonic on a regular basis.

When asked whether or not he thought of himself as a pioneer, his answer was 'no.' Mr. Allen said at this point he simply thought of himself as a young musician being given a chance to play in a first class orchestra. Once actually in the orchestra, he began to realize that the chance to be a pioneer had been thrust upon him.

In 1963 he was a participant in the Marlboro Music Festival.

Mr. Allen has performed many chamber music engagements as well as solo appearances with orchestras. He has appeared at Town Hall, Carnegie Recital Hall, Avery Fisher Hall, Alice Tully Hall as well as as a soloist with the Municipal Symphony Orchestra of New York, The New York Orchestral Society, The Symphony of the New World, The Baltimore Symphony, The Detroit Symphony and others. He has also performed in many places all over the world including the Virgin Islands, Belgium, France, and the Netherlands.

In addition to private teaching he is a former faculty member of Livingston College of Rutgers University: has served on an advisory panel of the New York State Council on the Arts and is currently a vice-chairman of the Advisory Commission of the High School of Performing Arts, in New York City.

In 1974 High School Fidelity Magazine awarded him the Koussevitzky International Recording Award.

In conjunction with the Society of Black Composers he has premiered numerous works by Black Composers.

13

I asked Mr. Allen what he felt could be done to improve the situation of the Black string instrumentalists. He replied that our Black Colleges must do something to raise the standard of teaching in the string department. Traditionally our vocal departments have been stronger than our string department. He felt that our Black Colleges must become involved in hiring more and better trained string teachers. He would like to teach in one of the predominantly black colleges eventually but at the moment does not want to leave the New York area.

When asked about teaching in a two year college he said that it would not be fair to the students or to him to try and prepare them in two years to compete with students who have trained for four years in a conservatory. He said, "two years is simply not enough time to give them a thorough training in the event the student does have talent."

Mr. Allen also said that strings are not very conducive to studying in a classroom and must also be studied privately. He explained that the success of the Yale School of Music and the Indiana School of Music in turning out good string instrumentalists is due largely to their very strong string faculties.

Sanford Allen is also a little disappointed that our black radio stations do not play more of the performances and compositions of some of our Black Musicians who are classically trained. Blacks have made tremendous contributions to the field of classical music. These contributions are very often overlooked by our Black radio announcers.

A modest man, he does not consider himself to be an established artist because he is not playing as much solo work, as he would like to.

I was curious about his impressions of the level of music in the black churches and why it has not aided in turning out a great many string instrumentalists.

He feels that the musical training of many of our ministers while in seminary is lacking, thereby causing many of them to choose poorly trained directors of music who in turn set up very poor music departments in many of our churches.

14

Another concept that Mr. Allen feels would help to produce more Black professional string players is exposure. He feels that one important factor in his own life was that as a child his parents took him to many concerts. He has tried very hard to do this with his own children and hopes that more black parents will try to do this with their children. I quote, "If a child is taken to concerts where he hears and sees violinist, the thought might occur to him, 'I can become a violinist.' Attitude is what molds the child, even more so than economics."

He went on to say that it is important to start students in the study of an instrument as early as possible. He said just how young is an individual thing. There have been some instances where a talented adult (under 30) began to study a string instrument and became a good instrumentalist even though not necessarily of professional caliber. Adults have the ability to concentrate when they practice whereas children are usually more easily sidetracked. The most important thing in studying an instrument is learning how to practice so that there is continuous growth.

He believes it is his responsibility as a Black musician to have some Black students. Some of his private students are Black.

As far as races are concerned, Mr. Allan thinks that the forms of racism have changed from the physical (e.g. lynching) to psychological (e.g. tokenism). He continued by saying that although 20 years ago there were no Black musicians playing in the major orchestras when one considers the ratio of Blacks to whites in this country there is no relationship between the percentage of Blacks in this country and the percentage of Blacks in the major orchestras. "How fair is tokenism?"

Mr. Allen stated that in this country there are still a lot of people with the state of mentality that says, 'I don't believe Blacks can play string instruments. '

I asked him why it has been very difficult for Black conductors in the country.
His answer was that a conductor is in a position of authority and many people don't want to see a black in position of authority.

In an article that he wrote for the New York Times that appeared in the Times on June 25, 1967, Mr. Allen stated the following ideas about the situation of Blacks in symphony orchestras:

15

Most of the major orchestra players have experience in smaller feeder orchestras. Most of these feeder orchestras are in small towns and the average Black has no desire to go in this type of town to play in a feeder orchestra. "There are other handicaps, 'such as not having studied with the right teachers or not having attended the 'right' conservatory, " Mr. Allen explains.

He further stated that there have often been board members who bring pressure on orchestras who are trying to hire Black conductors and instrumentalists or to play the music of Black Conductors. He pinpointed the problem of racial prejudice in the admittance of various conservatories. He also added that these racially biased admission procedures have been modified somewhat. Another hindrance is the 'dubious' manner in which orchestras hire their musicians. These dubious procedures help to disguise a racial prejudice used in hiring practices.

Another very interesting point that he made is, and I quote, "It seems to be absolutely necessary to involve all school children in projects which... lead[s] to a lack of qualification which, in turn, leads to statements by those who should know better that there is no talent and no interest on the part of members of minority groups. This is a situation, which needless to say, is certainly not restricted to the area of music. "

When asked about his goal, Mr. Allen shares that he intends to do more solo playing and make a greater impact on young black string players of today. He would eventually like to have enough money to set up competitions for young violinists this would be a way to help get more publicity for young upcoming minority violinists.

Also, it is important to note that Mr. Allen likes spirituals and is sad that they are rarely performed nowadays.

Mr. Allen has performed works by Coleridge-Taylor Perkinson, Noel Da Costa, Hale Smith, Dorothy Moore and other Black composers, has received honorable mention in High Fidelity Magazine and his hobbies are cooking and traveling.

For the moment he has one recording:
(Columbia - Black Composer series) Cordero - "Concerto for violin and Orchestra."

16

Marian Anderson
Photo courtesy ICM Artists, LTD
Sheldon Gold, President

18

Marian Anderson
Born 1901 – April 8, 1993
Contralto

Marian Anderson was born in South Philadelphia on Webster Street. She
began singing in the Union Baptist Church choir at the age of six. She
appeared in her first duet with another girl named viola Johnson during
her first year in the choir. Mr. Robinson was the director of music at her
church. He was not a trained musician and work for the church on a
voluntary basis.

Miss Anderson's father, John Anderson worked in the refrigeration room at
the Reading Terminal Market. He was also a coal and Ice dealer. On
Sundays he was the head usher at the church. Her mother, Annie
Anderson, was born in Lynchburg, Virginia and had been a school teacher.
Miss Anderson has two younger sisters Alyce and Ethel, respectively. At
the age of eight she began to teach herself the piano. She later tried to
teach herself the violin but gave up. While she was still eight, she
participated in a concert for the benefit of her church building fund. At age
10 her father died. Her mother began to take in wash because it was hard
for even professionally trained Negroes to find a good job because of
rampant racism. When she became 12 she began to help support the
family by doing Church concerts. At 13 she joined the senior choir of the
Union Baptist Church.

She began her secondary education at William Penn high school but later
transferred to South Philadelphia high school. While in high school, many
things began to happen that helped to get Marian Anderson's career
started: a friend of the family named John Thomas Butler used to give
readings in his spare time. He became interested in Miss Anderson's career
and introduced her to Mary Saunders Patterson, who became her friend
and voice teacher. Mrs. Patterson taught her for free. Miss Anderson
attempted to enroll in a music school but was discouraged by a girl in the
admissions office who told her that the school "did not take in colored."
Her second voice teacher was Agnes Reifsnyder.

19

The annual gala at her church, Union Baptist, was the annual Star Concert. At these Star Concerts Roland Hayes was always the featured artist. At one of these concerts her church invited her to perform on the program. This was an honor for an unknown Negro singer to perform on a program with Roland Hayes. Roland Hayes, upon hearing her sing, took an interest in Miss Anderson's career and recommended her to various colleges and churches in the area. He also suggested that she study voice with his voice teacher in Boston. However, her family would not allow her to go to Boston because she had no relatives living in the Boston area.

The principal at South Philadelphia high school also took an interest in her future and introduced her to Lisa Roma, who was a well-known opera star. Miss Roma took Marian Anderson to her voice teacher, Mr. Boghetti, and told Miss Anderson that she would "allow her five minutes of her precious time," in order to have her sing for Mr. Boghetti. Mr. Boghetti became Marion Anderson voice teacher and was the voice teacher from whom she received most of her vocal training. During this time miss Anderson became a member of the Philadelphia choral society, of which Alfred Hill was the director.

When she began to study with Mr. Boghetti, Miss Anderson did not have enough money to afford the lessons. Her church presented a quartet featuring Marian Anderson, as the contralto, and Roland Hayes, as the tenor, in a benefit performance of "In a Persian Garden." At this concert $600.00 was raised, which was used towards Miss Anderson lessons with Mr. Boghetti.

Shortly after she finished high school, G. Grant Williams, one of the editors of the Philadelphia Tribune, began to manage her concerts. This was a paper that served the Negro Community.

Not long after this, William King, who was Roland Haynes' former accompanist, became Miss Anderson's regular accompanist, and began to manage her concerts. While William King was managing her concerts, she did a concert at the Philadelphia Academy of Music. This was their first big venture. People were still calling for tickets until an hour before the concert. This was extremely exciting!

While Mr. King was still her manager, he booked her for a concert at Hampton Institute. R. Nathaniel Dett was chairman of the Music Department at Hampton Institute. He took an interest in Miss Anderson's career and at his insistence they were frequently invited back to perform at Hampton. This was not to say that the beauty of Miss Anderson's voice and her own hard work did not speak for themselves. Both the Philadelphia Academy concert and Hampton Institute were very important in establishing a concert circuit for her in this country. She and Mr. King also presented a concert at Howard University.

In 1921 she made her Town Hall debut. About this time she met the man who was to become her husband, Orpheus H. Fischer. But she did not marry him until sometime later.

Her first record was a recording of "Deep River "with "Heaven, Heaven" on the other side. They were both test records.

Her first First French coach was Miss Janey, whom she met through Mr. Boghetti. Her next French coach, Leon Rothier, who was a bass at the Metropolitan opera.

In 1926 she won the Philadelphia Philharmonic society contest. As a result of this contest, she made her first appearance with the Philadelphia Philharmonic society.

In 1925 300 performers participated in the Lewisohn Stadium contest, given by the New York Philharmonic Orchestra held at Aeolian Hall in New York. Marian Anderson won! She went on to make her debut with the New York Philharmonic on August 26, 1925 at Lewisohn Stadium, with William Van Hoogstraten as conductor.

Some time after, she appeared at Lewisohn Stadium with the Hall Johnson choir (see page 82) at Carnegie Hall. Author Judson became aware of Marian Anderson as a result of his appearance and became her manager.

Mr. Judson suggested that she study with Frank Laforge. She eventually did study with Mr. Laforge on a scholarship that was open in his studio.

Mr. Judson began to feel that, if she was ever to become an established singer, Miss Anderson must go to Europe. Therefore, she left for England. While there she studied German with Raimund Von ZurMuhlen and later with Mark Raphael. She also studied voice with Amanda Ira Aldrich, the daughter of the famous African Shakespearean actor, Ira Aldrich.

Miss Anderson gave her first European concert at Wigmore Hall in London. She sang at the promenade concerts in England on September 16, 1930, yet returned to the United States later that year still a relatively unknown singer.

In 1931 Miss Anderson went back to Europe this time to Germany through a Julius Rosenwald Scholarship. While there she studied Lieder with Michael Raucheisen. She sang her first concert in Germany at the Bachsaal.

Her early accompanist in Germany was Michael Raucheisen. She was managed in Germany by a Mr. Walter, who also arranged her Scandinavian concerts. While she was in Germany, a manager by the name of Rule Rasmussen and a young Finnish pianist named Kosti Vehanen, visited the studio where she was studying. These two gentlemen were to become her manager and accompanist when she returned to Scandinavia in 1933.

From Germany Miss Anderson went to Scandinavia under the management of Mr. Walter. She performed in Oslo, Stockholm, Helsinki, Stavanger, Bergen, and Copenhagen. Upon completion of the Scandinavian tour, she returned to the United States. Although this tour had been successful, she returned to the United States still a relatively unknown singer. In spite of her stellar performances and reviews, American critics did not feel that the Scandinavian audiences were as important as Parisan, London or Viennese audiences and therefore took scant notice of Miss Anderson's accomplishments.

In 1933 she returned to Scandinavia on the remaining part of her Julius Rosenwald Scholarship. There she performed 108 concerts that year. In Finland, she sang for Sibelius, the legendary Finnish composer. Sibelius said, "The roof of my house is too low for you."

Marian Anderson began to receive the recognition that she deserved. In 1934 Miss Anderson won the Grand Prix Du Chants for the best voice in Europe. In 1935 she sang in London and Paris. In Paris she performed at the prestigious concert hall, the Salle Gaveau. Finally, her third concert in Paris began to make Marian Anderson an established artist. American impresario, Sol Hurok attended this concert and he became Marian Anderson's manager that year. Miss Anderson sang in Brussels, Geneva, Vienna, and Salzburg. One of the most acclaimed musicians of all time, Arturo Toscanini was in the audience in Salzburg and said, "Yours is a voice such as one hears in a hundred years." This became public news instantly.

Miss Anderson returned to the United States and began to be offered concerts under Hurok's management in 1935. She performed her second Town Hall concert on December 10, 1935. The concert was an instant success.

In 1936 she sang at the Philadelphia Forum and then went to Russia. She performed in Leningrad, Tiflis, Moscow, Kiev, Krakow and Odessa.

In 1939 because of racism, the Daughters of the American Revolution, who owned the hall denied Miss Anderson use of Constitution Hall in Washington, D.C. As a result of this, Mrs. Franklin D. Roosevelt withdrew from the organization. Many were offended. Mr. Hurok arranged for a concert to take place on the steps of the Lincoln Memorial on Easter Sunday morning, April 9, 1939. Miss Anderson made history when 75,000 people attended this monumental event. Most people do not know that shortly before this concert, Kosti Vehanen, who had been her accompanist for some time, became ill. Franz Rupp was rushed out to Washington, D.C. to take over. While she was under Hurok management, Mr. Rupp remained her accompanist for the next 25 years

Also during the 1939 season she was invited, through the head of the Howard University Music Department, by Mrs. Eleanor Roosevelt to sing at the White House, and she performed for King George II and the Queen of England. When Miss Anderson performed in Tokyo, Mrs. Roosevelt also attended that concert.

From then on, whenever Miss Anderson found out that Mrs. Roosevelt would be occupying the same hotel room right after her, she would leave notes of greetings for her in on the mirror.

23

In 1941 she won the Edward Bok Award which is given annually to a Philadelphian who has helped to bring distinction to the City. She received $10,000 and a disc. With this $10,000 Miss Anderson created the Marian Anderson Scholarship fund.

In 1942 after a concert in Wilmington, Delaware, Marian Anderson married the architect, Orpheus H. Fischer.

In 1943 she won the order of African Redemption, which is the highest honor that the Liberian Government can bestow.

In 1947 she made a tour of the West Indies.

She has also performed at Convent Garden in London, England.

On January 7, 1955 she made her Metropolitan Opera Debut in the part of Ulrica in "A Masked Ball" by Verdi and became the first Negro to sing at the Metropolitan. Robert McFerrin became a member of the Metropolitan Opera Company that same year (see page 100).

In 1965 she gave up concert tours.

She also studied voice with Edyth Walker, Steffi Rupp, who was the wife of Franz Rupp, and Madame Freschel.

Among some of the other appearances she has made are: performances in Tel Aviv, Israel, and for the Empress of Japan. She has also appeared in a benefit concert arranged by Mayor Fiorello La Guardia.

Marian Anderson's awards include: one from the Government of Sweden: The Order of the White Rose from the Government of Finland; Honorary Degrees from: Howard University, Temple University, Smith, Carlisle, Moravian, Fairleigh Dickson and Duke University; The Spingarn Medal from the NAACP; The Philadelphia Award and the Key to Atlantic City.

Her hobbies are: sewing, gardening, cooking, and refinishing old furniture.

Miss Anderson has written her autobiography entitled, "My Lord What a Morning."

Her records include:

24

"Marian Anderson Sings Beloved Songs by Schubert" (RCA Victor)
"   "   "   Lieder by Schuman" (RCA Victor)
"   "   "   Lieder by Brahms" (RCA Victor)
"   "   "   Lieder by Strauss" (RCA Victor)
"   "   "   Sacred Arias by Bach" (RCA Victor)
"   "   "   Christmas Carols" (RCA Victor)
"   "   "   Old American Songs" (RCA Victor)
"   "   "   Operatic Arias" (RCA Victor)
"   "   "   Spirituals" (RCA Victor)
"Songs at Eventide" (RCA Victor)

"The Alto Rhapsody" by Brahms (RCA Victor)

"Marian Anderson Farewell Recital" (RCA Victor)

25

Martina Arroyo

Martina Arroyo

Martina Arroyo was born in New York City. Her father Demetrio Arroyo was an engineer. Her mother, Lucille Washington Arroyo was born and educated in Charleston, South Carolina. Demetrio Arroyo and Lucille W. Arroyo were married for 42 years before he died. Miss Arroyo has one older brother, Reverend Theodore W. Kerrison, who was the pastor of St. Augustine Baptist Church, in Bronx, New York. Miss Arroyo grew up in Harlem.

Miss Arroyo attended Hunter High School and Hunter College where she majored in romance languages and minored in education. Privately Miss Arroyo pursued her music studies, as well as studying German. She did her graduate work at New York University.

Upon receiving her bachelor's degree, she started a teaching career. After two semesters she also worked as a caseworker in Manhattan and was assigned a caseload of 110 families.

She made her debut in 1958 at Carnegie Hall in the concert version of the opera "Murder in the Cathedral" by Pizzetti.

Urged by her voice teacher, Madame Marinka Gurenwich, to enter the 1958 Metropolitan Opera auditions, she won the auditions. In 1959 Miss Arroyo made her debut as the offstage celestial voice in Verdi's "Don Carlo." She has gone on to achieve a great deal of fame as one of the few black singers to ever become a regular member of the Metropolitan Opera Company. Martina Arroyo has also sung with the Hamburg State Opera, the Berlin State Opera, the Cologne and the Frankfurt Operas, La Scala in Milan, Convent Garden in London, the Paris Opera, the Rome Opera, The Stockholm Opera, the Vienna State Opera, the Teatro colon in Buenos Aires, at the Salzburg Festival and throughout Yugoslavia.

In 1963 she made her New York Philharmonic debut in "Andromache's Farewell" by Samuel Barber, which was subsequently recorded.

In 1963 she married Emilio Poggioni, who is a concert violinist. He has performed concerts throughout Europe, the United States and the far east with the Societa Caremistica Italiana and Trio di Como.

Martina Arroyo is an extremely versatile musician and has also become well known for her interpretation of contemporary works, in addition to her performances of the standard operatic repertoire. Among the contemporary performances she has sung are:
"Offrandes" by Edgar Varese and "An Mathilde" by Luigi Dallapiccola, the latter work was performed under the baton of Leonard Bernstein. Composer Karlheinz Stockhausen asked Miss Arroyo to perform the world premiere of his cantata "Momente." She later presented the United States premiere of this cantata.

In 1970 she opened the Metropolitan Opera in Verdi's "Ernani", and 1971 in Verdi's "Don Carlo", making this two consecutive opening nights, achieved only by six other leading sopranos in the history of the Metropolitan Opera.

Besides performing in opera, Miss Arroyo is well known for her interpretation of Lieder.

Her recordings include:

"Les Huguenots" by Meyerbeer (London)
"La Forza del Destino" by Verdi (Angel)
"Siciliani" by Verdi (RCA)
"Don Giovanni" by Mozart (Donna Elvira) (Deutsche Grammophon)
         "   "   "   (Donna Anna) (Phillips)
        "La Juive" by Halevy (excerpts)
        "Requiem" by Verdi (Leonard Bernstein conducting) (Columbia)
        "Missa Solemnis" by Beethoven (Ormandy) (Columbia)
        "Spirituals" (conducted by Dorothy Maynor)
        "Requiem" by Faure, (conducted by Frederic Walsmann)
(Columbia)
        "Ninth Symphony" by Beethoven (conducted by Bernstein)
(Columbia)
        "Eighth Symphony" , (conducted by Rafael Kubelik) (Deutshe
Grammophon)
        "Stabat Mater" by Rossini (Schippers-N.Y. Philharmonic)
(Columbia)

28

Grace Bumbry in the role of Tosca
Picture courtesy Metropolitan Opera Archives
Louis Milancon, Photographer

Grace Bumbry
January 4, 1937 –

(She began her career as a mezzo-soprano but now classified as a soprano.)

Miss Bumbry was born in St.Louis, Missouri, the youngest in the family of three children. She was the only daughter. Her father, Benjamin James Bumbry was a freight handler for the railroad. Her mother Melzia Walker Bumbry (from whom Miss Bumbry gets her middle name, Melzia) was a schoolteacher from Mississippi. Her brothers names are Benjamin and Charles.

She first sang in the choir at Union Methodist Church in St. Louis. She attended Sumner High School in her hometown. After Miss Bumbry won the Arthur Godfrey Talent Scouts, she attended Boston University and Northwestern University as a voice major.

In 1956 she went to the Academy of the West to study with Lotte Lehmann and became her protégé.

In 1958 she won $1000 as a finalist in the Metropolitan Opera Competition.

In 1959 Miss Bumbry went to Europe to seek her fortune. While singing at the Festival in Bayreuth, Grace Bumbry gained the distinction of becoming the first Black singer to sing the role of Venus in "Tannhauser." This role made her an established singer. While in Europe for three years she was a regular member of the Opera Company in Basel, Switzerland.

In 1962 Miss Bumbry was invited to sing at the White House by Mrs. Jacqueline Kennedy. During the same year she also made her Carnegie Hall Debut.

In 1963 Miss Bumbry sang with the Lyric Opera Company of Chicago in the roles of Venus in "Tannhauser" and Ulrica in "A Masked Ball." Later that same year she went to Switzerland and while there married Erwin Andreas Jaeckel, a Polish tenor. They are now divorced.

Miss Bumbry has been the recipient of the following awards:
- Kimber Foundation Award, San Francisco

30

- National Marian Anderson Award
- John Hay Whitney Foundation
- First Prize, Metropolitan opera Auditions of the Air
- California Federation of Teachers of Singing

Miss Bumbry has also sung at the Paris Opera, La Scala in Milan, the Staatsoper in Vienna, La Monnaie in Brussels, Teatro dell 'Opera in Rome, Teatro San Carlo in Naples, Teatro Comunale in Bologna, Teatro Colon in Buenos Aires, The Salzburg Festival in Salzburg; in Japan, Stockholm, Helsinki, Copenhagen, Belgrade, Berlin, Munich, Hamburg, Cologne, etc. etc.

Discography:
"Carmen Jones"
Angel Records: 'Brahms, Five Songs, Schubert, Five Songs, Schumann, Five Songs' (Lieder Recital)
                'Casta Diva" Italian Operatic Arias
                "Carmen" complete opera
                "Orfeo" highlights and complete performance
                "Mozart Requiem"
                "Aida" complete performance and highlights
                "The Gypsy's Baron" by Johann Strauss

Westminster: "Israel in Egypt" by Handel
                "Judas Maccabaeus" by Handel

London Records: "Messiah" by Handel
                "Don Carlo" complete

Deutsche Gramophone Records: Verdi Arias
                "Zigeunerlieder" by Brahms

Philips Records: "Tannhauser" Bayreuth Festival performance, complete

RCA Records: "Aida" complete and highlights

Henry T. Burleigh
Picture courtesy ASCAP

Henry Thacker Burleigh
(Also known as Harry Thacker Burleigh)
December 2, 1866 – September 15, 1949
Composer, Instrumentalist, Singer

This is one of the only two sketches in this book for which the next of kin
could not be reached. The information in the sketch was for the most part
verified by the American Society of Composers Authors and Publishers
(ASCAP). I have indicated those places where I disagree with ASCAP and
stated my other sources.

Henry T. Burleigh sang baritone, composed, and played the piano, double
bass and timpani.

Mr. Burleigh was born in Erie, Pennsylvania. Burleigh's father, Henry T.
Burleigh Sr. died when Burleigh was quite young. One source said that he
was blind. I do not share this opinion because some years later when
Burleigh was asked about his family background he mentioned that his
grandfather had been blind and that as a small boy he had led him around
by the hand. He made no mention of his father ever having been blind.

Burleigh's mother, Elizabeth Waters Burleigh was a college graduate. After
her husband's death she took a job as a janitress at a public school
because there were not that many good jobs for Black professional at the
time. Her father was a blind slave who had used the Underground Railroad
to escape to the north. It was this man that Burleigh referred to when
speaking of his childhood.

Burleigh did various jobs to help support himself. Among these were desk
steward and lamplighter. Burleigh sang so well that he won a scholarship
to the National Conservatory in New York. I feel that we should mention
something about the circumstances that surrounded Burleigh's entrance
into the New York Conservatory for reasons that will become obvious in
due time.

While Burleigh was still a young boy his mother found it necessary to take on additional work while working as a janitress. As a result, she started doing housework for a wealthy white woman. This lady sometimes entertained various well-known musicians at her home. But amazingly Mr. Burleigh's mother would tell him when the gatherings were to take place so that he could stand outside the window and listen. At one of these gatherings while he stood in the snow and listened, he contracted pneumonia. Upon hearing this the lady of the household, gave him the job of doorboy so that he could listen and be inside. Burleigh met many notable people at these gatherings. Later at the New York Conservatory even after he had passed the auditions there were still some members of the board who still did not want to admit him. The final outcome was determined by one lady he had met in his capacity as door boy. She used her influence to help him gain admittance to the Conservatory in spite of the fact that he had already proven his ability. Burleigh entered the school in 1892.

Burleigh spent four years at the Conservatory, two of which he spent in the teaching of piano and solfeggio. While there he studied harmony with the Ruben Goldmark , counterpoint with Max Spick, voice with Christian Fritsch and orchestration with composer and conductor, Frank Van der Stucken.

It was at this point in Burleigh's life that he met Anton Dvorak who had become director of the Conservatory. Burleigh helped to inspire Dvorak's interest in Afro-American Spirituals. Later when he composed his "New World Symphony" (first performed in 1893) he used the spiritual "Swing Low, Sweet Chariot" which had been introduced to him by Burleigh. (ASCAP shares this opinion about "Swing Low, Sweet Chariot".)

As for the theme of the "Largo" there are different schools of thought. The American Society of Composers Authors and Publishers (ASCAP) believe this was an original theme written by Dvorak himself.

I do not share this opinion. I also feel, as do some other musicians that this was also a spiritual, which Dvorak arranged for use in his symphony.

34

Maude Cuney-Hare in her book "Negro Musicians and their Music" published by Da Capo Press, NY had a letter reproduced that was written by Burleigh in 1918. I quote, "There is a tendency in these days to ignore the Negro elements in the 'New World Symphony' shown by the fact that many of those who were able in 1893 to find traces of Negro musical color all through the symphony ... now cannot find anything in the whole four movements that suggest any local of Negro influence.. There is no doubt that Dvorak was deeply impressed by the old Negro 'Spirituals' and also by Foster's songs... And one in particular 'Swing Low, Sweet Chariot' greatly pleased him...."

At the conclusion of Burleigh's letter the following quote appears, 'Miss Alice Fletcher claims, that she heard the Indians sing the theme of the 'Largo' at a time when they had no borrowed music. As the Indians and Negroes inter-married (either with or without the sanction of the church), in both New England and the South, during the earliest days in America, one may find themes borrowed from the Negro. The Indian folk song is markedly unmelodic."

In 1894 Burleigh won a competition over 60 other singers and obtained the post of baritone soloist of St. George's Church on Stuyvesant Square in New York City.

In 1898 he married Louise Alston who later bore his one son, Saptian Alston Waters Burleigh.

Burleigh joined the choir at Temple Emanuel and was the only Afro-American ever to have sung in the Synagogue.

In 1971 he received the Spingarn Award. This award is given for outstanding contributions to civil rights by the National Association for the Advancement of Colored People (NAACP).

A charter member of the American Society of Composers Authors and Publishers (ASCAP), in 1941 he was the first Black to be nominated for a seat on its board of directors.

Burleigh sang in Hebrew, Latin, French, German, and Italian.

35

During the course of his concertizing he sang for Theodore Roosevelt, The ArchBishop of Canterbury, Prince Henry of Prussia, Paderewski, Anton Seidl and in a command performance for Edward VII. He also went on lecture tours with Booker T. Washington and sang duets with Roland Hayes. (See page 78)

One of the pioneers for setting down the Afro-American Spirituals on paper, Burleigh arranged more than 100 Spirituals. Additionally, he composed more than 250 original songs. Most of his original compositions took the form of semi-classical ballads. He also wrote several anthems as well as pieces for the violin.

He served as the musical editor for G. Ricordi and Sons as well as the New York City Music Publishers Co.

Henry T. Burleigh was a multi-faceted musician and strived to make a record of the link between our music here and the music of Africa: "The Spirituals".

His last residence was at 823 West 166 Street New York City on edge of Harlem.

Some of his better-known arrangements are:
"Deep River" Solo (pub. Belwin Mills, Melville, New York)
" "   Choral (pub. G. Schirmer, New York)
" I Stood On De Ribber Ob Jerdon" Choral (Belwin Mills etc.)
" I Been In De Storm So Long Children" solo --------------

I should add that although various other editors have re-edited some of Mr. Burleigh's choral arrangements since his death, if these choral arrangements are performed a capella without these various added accompaniments, the "flavor" of the spiritual style of singing comes through more clearly. I am sure that this is more in keeping with what Mr. Burleigh had in mind.

John Childs

John Childs
October 4, 1932 –
Composer, Pianist

Some months ago I was attending a delightful concert by the soprano, Mareda Gather Graves, at the Brooks Memorial United Methodist Church in Queens, New York. Towards the middle of the concert the singer changed accompanists for several pieces written by John Childs. Upon further scrutiny of the program I found that the new accompanist was the composer himself. I must confess that as a professional musician I have not always been able to understand the music of many of our contemporary "Classical "musicians. A Bach score is far easier for me to grasp than a Stravinsky score. However I was so swept up by the lyricism of the music that I found it easy to grasp in spite of the idiom. I determined that I must find out more about the composer. John Childs is not as well-known or as established as the other composers contained herein but I believe that his music will withstand the test of time and that he should be mentioned here.

John Childs was born in Baltimore, Maryland. His father, John Childs, Senior and mother Emily Britain Childs were also born in Baltimore. He has one brother, Avon, who was named for Avon Long.

When he was four years old he began to study piano privately with L. Ellsworth Tooney and continued to do so until he was 14. At eight years of age he began to compose. When he was 11 years old he began to sing in the Baltimore Boys Choir and continue to do so for 3 1/2 years.

At 14 he entered the Baltimore Institute of Musical Arts. This was a fairly new conservatory at the time and had only been in existence for a few years. With preparation from the Baltimore Institute of Musical Arts he entered the Juilliard School of Music. He majored in piano while attending Juilliard and while there studied piano with Alton Jones. He graduated from Juilliard with an Artist Diploma in 1955.

Between 1961 and 1963 he studied composition privately with Lee Hoiby.

Mr. Childs has spent a great deal of his career accompanying ballet classes at establish schools on piano. At present he is the piano accompanist for the Harkness School for Ballet Arts.

He was director of a children's choir at the Mace School for 10 years. This was a private school for children in the entertainment world. Some of the students that this school produced are: Lynn Loring, and Carol Lynley and Hines of Hines, Hines.

His works have been performed by the Harlem Chorale: Mareda Gather Graves, who is a member of the faculty of Ithaca College; Fred Thomas, Francis Walker, Miriam Burton and the Carr-Hill Singers.

On May 23, 1976 the Carr-Hill Singers premiered one of his choral pieces at the Brooks Memorial United Methodist Church.

On May 26,1976, a tenor, John Stenson performed 5 pieces for voice and piano at the New York University School of Education: "Songs" 1963-1964

Mr. Childs feels like his two most representative works are "E'tenebris" 1965; and "Songs" 1963-1964.

His output is small at this time and he feels that it is not truly representative of all he hopes to do. John Childs says his biggest problem is getting commissions and finding more groups to perform his works. He believes that his productivity will increase as channels for performing increase.

At present he has three recordings:

Ballet Album 1967 (Hoctor)
Ballet II 1968 (Hoctor)
"Andalusian and Flamenco Dances" 1974 (the music on this album is both original and adapted. It was done with the total collaboration of Mariquita Flores.)

Gloria Davy in the role of Aida
Picture courtesy Metropolitan Opera Archives

40

Gloria Davy
March 29, 1931-November 28, 2012
Soprano

Gloria Davy was born in Brooklyn, New York. Her parents George and Lucy Davy were from the island of St. Vincent. She had two sisters Dorothy and Lillian and one brother Edward J. One curious fact is that her family is not musically inclined. Miss Davey stands 5 feet 8 inches tall.

The recipient of the Marian Anderson Award in 1951 and 1952, Miss Davy graduated from the High School of Music and Art in New York City. She later attended Juilliard and graduated with a Bachelor of Science with a major in Music.

Miss Davy then began a career as a concert singer. She won the vocal competition of Music Educators League in 1954. First prize was a Town Hall Debut and that same year Miss Davy was a soloist with the Little Orchestra Society. Also during 1954, Miss Davy succeeded Leontyne Price as Bess in Gershwin's "Porgy and Bess" and toured in the role in the United States, Canada, Europe. This tour included memorable performances at La Scala in Milan, Italy, Cairo, Egypt and in other parts of Northern Africa.

When the tour finished in 1955, Miss Davy settled in Milan and her fame as a concert and Lieder singer began to grow. She performed her first "Aida" at the Opera House in Nice, France.

In 1957 she signed a contract with the Metropolitan Opera Company. She later became the first Black to sing the role of "Aida" at the Metropolitan Opera House. In addition to "Aida" she also sang Leonora in "Il Trovatore," Pamina in "The Magic Flute" and Nedda in "Pagliacci."

In 1958 Miss Davy gave a recital at Carnegie Hall in New York City.

In 1960 she sang with the Philadelphia Orchestra under the Baton of Eugene Ormandy. During that same year she sang at La Scala in Milan; Town Hall in New York City as well as in Aachen, Germany.

She sang in a performance of "Cosi fan tutte" in Tel Aviv, Israel in 1961.

41

Miss Davy has sung the role of Aida with the Berlin Opera Company. She has also sung in Yugoslavia. She has performed with the American Opera Society.

The Brilliance of her "Aida" has spread throughout the music world, and she sang the part recently with Karajan at the Vienna State Opera; in Covent Garden in London and at the Duestche Opera Berlin in the famous Weiland Wagner production.
Today, Miss Davy's concert and opera repertoire ranges from Purcell, Handel, Gluck and Mozart to Rossini, Donizetti, Verdi, Puccini and Strauss. She is an accomplished interpreter of the modern literature. In 1972, she sang in the world premiere of Karlheinz Stockhausen's complete "Moment" cycle with the Cologne Radio Orchestra under the composer's baton and toured the major European capitals in "Momente."

On October 18, 1974, Miss Davy sang another Stockhausen world premiere; on that occasion she sang his "Inori" (Japanese for adoration), which was performed by the Donaueschingen Festival in West Germany. On October 22, she repeated the "Inori" in Paris and then on the 25th in London.

Gloria Davy is a favorite guest on internationally broadcast European television shows, including a telecast of Hindemith's "Des Todes Tod" that originated in Frankfurt. She taped a special for the prestigious CBS series, "Camera Three," while on a tour in New York with the Buffalo Philharmonic led by Lukas Foss. The tour climaxed with her singing Arnold Schoenberg's "Erwartung" at Carnegie Hall. She also played a leading role in a film on Arnold Schoenberg that had its world premiere during the 1974 Vienna Festival as part of the Schoenberg exhibition to commemorate the 100th anniversary of the composer's birth.

Miss Davy regularly tours major European countries, including Italy and West Germany, in recital, as a concert and oratorio singer.

Her discography includes:

(Deustche Grammophon)	"Moment" by Stockhausen
" "	"Aida" by Verdi, directed by Von Karajan
(Vox)	"Chimney" by Shulamit Ran
"	"Picnic Cantata" by Paul Bowles
(London)	"Gloria Davy Concert Recital"

William L. Dawson
Picture Courtesy New York Public Library, Lincoln Center

William Levi Dawson
September 25, 1899 - May 2, 1990
Composer, Trombonist, Conductor

William Levi Dawson was born in Anniston, Alabama. As a boy he shined shoes until he had saved enough money to go to Tuskegee Institute. At this point he ran away from home. After arriving at Tuskegee Institute in Tuskegee, Alabama he supported himself by working on a farm. In time he began to work in the various divisions of the agricultural department of Tuskegee. All the while studying various instruments, singing in the choir and studying harmony and piano.

He studied composition and orchestration at Washburn College in Topeka in 1921. From there he went to the Horner Institute of Fine Arts in Kansas City, Kansas where he majored in theory and counterpoint. After four years of study at the Horner Institute he received his bachelor of music degree.

From 1921 to 1922 Dawson served as director of music at the Kansas Vocational Institute in Topeka, Kansas.

From 1922 to 1926 Mr. Dawson served as director of music at Lincoln High School in Kansas City, Missouri.

He earned his master's degree in composition at the American Conservatory of Music in Chicago. While at the American Conservatory he began to play first trombone with the Chicago Civic Orchestra and became the first Black to play in the Orchestra.

He later became Director of Music at the Tuskegee Institute and directed the choir there for 25 years. During this time he made many concert tours across the country and several recordings. He made the Tuskegee Institute Choir, an established choir.

He wrote one of the first symphonies to be based solely upon Afro-American Spirituals called the "The Negro Symphony." This work was first performed on November 20, 1934 by the Philadelphia Orchestra under the baton of Leopold Stokowski.

Mr. Dawson has also written numerous choral arrangements of the Spirituals. Two of his better-known arrangements are: "There is a Balm in Gilead" publisher, Tuskegee Institute Press (Neil A. Kjos, Park Ridge, Illinois sole selling agent) and "Soon Ah Will Be Done" Tuskegee Institute Press (Neil A. Kjos etc.)

Some of the other publishers that publish some of his works are:

H.T. Fitzsimmons Co., Chicago, Illinois
Shawnee Press Inc., Delaware Water Gap, Pennsylvania

His discography includes:
(Decca)   "The Negro Folk Symphony" The American Symphony Orchestra, Stokowski conducting

(Westminster) "Spirituals" Tuskegee Institute Choir, Dawson conducting

The above recordings can be purchased from the:
Petite Bazaar Tuskegee Institute, Alabama. I believe this is a store on the campus, which is run by the composer and his relatives.

Leonard DePaur
Susanne Faulkner Stevens, Photographer

Leonard DePaur
November 18,1914 - November 7,1998
Conductor, Composer, Bass-Baritone, Lecturer, Writer

Leonard DePaur was born in Summit, New Jersey. He jokingly said that he was too old to list his date of birth. He said that his approximate age was in the fifties, which would put his date of birth sometime in the 1920s.

His Father, Ernst DePaur was born in the French West Indies. After his father moved here he continued to practice law and eventually went into politics. Leonard DePaur also informed me that his father was also quite musical and had a lovely bass voice.

Leonard DePaur's mother, Hettie Carson DePaur was born in South Carolina. A housewife as well as an amateur musician, Mrs. DePaur played the piano and sang. Leonard DePaur had a brother who had died in infancy and two sisters, one of whom had died a few years ago.

He is married to the former Norma Louise Childs. They have two children, Norma Lynn, who is a senior as Stamford College and Leonard Childs, who is a sophomore at Amherst College. Both of these young people are musical.

Leonard DePaur began his high school education at the historic Manual Training and Industrial School for Colored Youth in Bordentown, New Jersey where he continued his musical studies. While there he and some other boys organized a little jazz combo for which he played Saxophone. When they were no longer satisfied with the arrangements they could find, Leonard DePaur began to write arrangements for the group. This was the beginning of his career as an arranger and composer.

The Bordentown School was a specialized school and taught various trades. Music was one of the trades that they taught. Mr. DePaur informed me that they had an excellent music faculty. The school was a boarding school and run in military fashion.

47

A very interesting incident happened while Mr. DePaur was a student at the Manual Training School. The young DePaur used to make extra money by pawning items from the other boys. One day one of the other boys said that he was going to get a trumpet for Christmas. The other boys all believed him and nothing more was said. In actuality the boy was joining the school band and was going to be issued a trumpet by the school. Upon receiving the trumpet from the school, the boy pawned it to Leonard DePaur in order to have money for the weekend. When the weekend was over the boy went back to the young DePaur for the trumpet. When DePaur asked for his money with the agreed interest the boy said that he would be getting some money soon and could he have the trumpet. The young DePaur refused whereupon the boy told the school authorities. The Commander sent for DePaur and reprimanded him. He then gave young DePaur an hour to change his mind. DePaur, even at this point, being a man of conviction, would not give in. Leonard DePaur was placed on a six-month suspension and sent home.

Once out of high school, Mr. DePaur began to look for various ways of expressing his music. One day while attending a show at a Loew's theater an usher was led down the aisle to sing in between features. The Young DePaur realizing that the boy's voice was not as good as his own wasted no time telling the manager that he was sure he could sing better than the fellow he had heard that evening. The manager auditioned Leonard DePaur and informed him that he was right.

He was given a job as a porter in the theater (the only job Blacks could hold in a theater at the time) and sang in between features from then on.

One day a managing agent heard him and informed him that he could get him better vaudeville bookings and more money. Leonard DePaur went under his management and began to launch a successful career as a vaudeville singer.

48

He was eventually introduced to Hall Johnson and invited to one of Mr. Johnson's rehearsals with the famed Hall Johnson Choir. The Young DePaur was overwhelmed by what he heard and saw that night and decided to join the choir. (See page 82) In many ways, Hall Johnson played a pivotal part in Leonard DePaur's growth and development. Hall Johnson succeeded in convincing Leonard DePaur to complete his high school education and with Hall Johnson he studied composition and orchestration as well as the interpretation of the Afro-American Spiritual. Additionally, while studying with Hall Johnson, Leonard DePaur met and befriended another student of Johnson's, Jester Hairston, a composer, songwriter and leading expert on Negro Spirituals.

After Leonard DePaur left the Hall Johnson Choir, he continued his composition studies with Henry Cowell, the composer and impresario. He then entered the Juilliard School of Music as a composition student. While at Juilliard he also studied conducting with Albert Stoessel. He did further undergraduate work at Columbia University and at the L' Universite Laval in France where he studied conducting with Pierre Monteux.

Mr. DePaur has been awarded an Honorary Doctor of Music Degree by Lewis and Clark College. In addition to his other training he has also studied voice privately with Sergei Radamsky, who was a Russian Tenor. He has also studied with John Patterson. Another person who gave him a great deal of information about voice but with whom he never studied was Leon Rothier. Leon Rothier was the Metropolitan Opera bass who was asked to substitute for Ezio Pinza on various occasions.

In 1942 he joined the army.

In 1946 he joined the Infantry Chorus of the 322nd Infantry Regiment -- this was an all Black regiment from the east coast. There are several interesting facts about the chorus. It was one of the few concertizing male choruses in the country at the time. In fact, it became one of the few professional male choruses that this country produced during that era. The most interesting fact about the infantry chorus was that the men all developed such a sense of loyalty to chorus that some of them extended their time in the army so that they could all come out together and continue concertizing.

49

The members of the 322nd Infantry Chorus all got out in 1947 and started to concertize professionally. At this point the name of the chorus was changed from 322nd infantry Chorus to The DePaur Infantry Chorus. The DePaur Infantry Chorus continued concertizing until 1956.

I asked Mr. DePaur why they ceased to exist after 1956. He explained that by 1956 the Korean war had already taken place and the songs of World War II were beginning to sound dated to them. Moreover that army had changed and their concert uniforms, which had evolved from the World War II Army Uniform were also beginning to look a little dated. One other unique fact about the DePaur Infantry Chorus is that it had several men with beautiful falsetto (For our purposes, the ability to imitate the voices sung by women, girls and young boys.) as well as one counter-tenor. (A man whose voice has never changed and he continus to sing a treble voice throughout his life.) (See glossary) This enabled him to do compositions for treble voices, mature male voices and mixed voices. With the DePaur Infantry Chorus Leonard DePaur toured South America, Germany, The Orient and the Caribbean.

At that point in his career he decided he would create an organization with an entirely different personality and repertoire. Thus in 1957 he formed the DePaur Opera Gala. This was a small operatic company in its own right and its repertoire was devoted solely to operatic music. He decided that this repertoire was a little too confining and its name was changed to the DePaur Gala in order to allow them to include works outside the operatic repertoire. Among the singers who performed with this organization were Lawrence Winters and Inez Matthews. The DePaur Gala toured Canada and the United States. This organization existed until 1960.

In 1963 Leonard DePaur was asked by several important people in the music world if he would consider organizing another male chorus. As a result of this conversation The DePaur Male Chorus was formed. This was a chorus with a repertoire drawn entirely from the standard repertoire. He explained that he made a point of doing things that were "miles away" from the repertoire of the DePaur Infantry Chorus in order to prevent any confusion of their identities. The DePaur Male Chorus toured South America; 15 countries in Africa; and France. It was an extremely successful chorus. This organization performed its last concert season in 1968.

In 1970 he took the post of Director of Community Relations for Lincoln Center. His primary function was to be the coordinator of the International College Choral Festival, which was to involve 40 choirs from around the world in a program of 16 concerts in various parts of the country. He had promised himself that he did not want to remain there past the completion of the first festival, which took place in 1972. He was intent upon getting back on the road on a permanent basis. The first festival was a success and the next one took place in 1974. He is still in Community Relations at Lincoln Center and makes various lectures and guest conducting appearances around the country whenever time permits.

He has lectured at the University of Rochester; Olympia College, The University of California, The New York State Historical Association and many other places.

He has guest conducted the musical, "Purlie" while it was on Broadway as well as on national tour. He has also served as the musical director for the Federal Theater Project-The Negro Theater. This theater was part of the Works Progress Administration (WPA) program.

He has been a member of the summer faculties of Kent State University-Blossom Festival, University of Colorado, University of the State of Washington, and Lewis and Clark College.

In addition to his other activities, he is the consultant for The Group "W" Network for the program "Black Pride"; New York City Board of Education CHIP Program; The Westport Summer Music Program; Cultural Development for the Republic of Tunisha; and Co-Chairman of the American Committee for the festival of Negro Art to be held in Dakar, Senegal.

His performance career has also included singing and acting on radio. He has been the arranger for 10 Broadway musicals, arranged and conducted single albums with Leontyne Price and Shirley Verrett and researched, arranged and directed a five album Anthology of Afro-American Folk Music for RCA. He served for a while as the arranger-conductor for the "Hallmark Hall of Fame", for which he received an Emmy nomination. He has arranged for the Bell Telephone Hour Chicago Series. He has conducted various commercial announcements for T.V. and radio for J. Walter Thompson Company and Ted Bates and Company.

51

He functioned in the capacity of writer-commentator for the "Music Makers 1969" for WQXR Radio. Leonard DePaur has served as arranger-conductor for 100 other radio programs on large networks. He has served as conductor-arranger for various films for 20th – Century Fox , Paramount and MGM studios.

His works have been published by the following firms:

Choral Series – Lawson Gould Music. (An affiliate of G. Schirmer)
Michael Brant Publications
Ameican Book Company – Choral Art Series
Elsa-Childs Music Publishing Company
Clara Music Publishing Company (Belafonte Enterprises)

Among his many awards are the following:

Harlem Historical Landmarks Foundation Award
An Award from the Clipper Club for the "The Furthering of International Understanding"
The Harold Jackman Memorial Committee Achievement Award (this award has also been received by Geoffrey Holder and other such celebrities.)
An award from the St. Marks Church of New York City
An award from the Church on the Hill of New York City

He is a member of the following organizations:
ASCAP
National Association for American Composers and Conductors
American Symphony Orchestra League
National Academy of Television Arts and sciences
Society of Black Composers
The Bohemians
American Veteran Committee
Aircraft Owner/Pilots Association
Sigma Pi Phi Fraternity, Zeta Boule

Mr. DePaur has received press in the following publications:
Time Magazine
Newsweek
Saturday Review
Negro Digest
Opera News
Ebony

Jet
Musical America
Musical Courier
Diapason
Etude
Who's Who
Colliers
Pathfinders
Essence

The giant personality is squeezed into a frame that is 5 feet 8 inches tall. However, one feels the size of the personality within a matter of minutes. A warm person with a tremendous love for music, people and a good conversation, such is Leonard DePaur.

Below is a sampling of his recordings:

United artists Records: (Current release) featuring Brock Peters and Odetta

Columbia Masterworks Records: "Sound – Off"   The DePaur Infantry Chorus (Plus nine other albums in this series)

Phillips- Mercury Records: (Two albums) DePaur Infantry Chorus

RCA Anthology of Afro-American Folk Music   (Five Albums)

He has other recordings in which he has conducted opera, as well as children's material, and a wide range of other materials.

Some of his more popular choral arrangements are as follows:

"In Bright Mansions Above" Pub. Lawson Gould, N.Y.C.
"Jesus Hung and Died" "   "   "   "
"City Call Heaven"   ---------------------------

R. Nathaniel Dett
Picture courtesy ASCAP

Robert Nathaniel Dett
October 11, 1882- October 2, 1943
Composer, Conductor, Pianist

This is the only sketch in the book other than the one on Harry T. Burleigh for which the next of kin could not be reached. In order to verify the information in this sketch I had to compare this information with research published by Domique-Rene DeLerma and other information published by Maude Cuney-Hare.

Dett was born in Drummondsville, Ontario, Canada. Drummondsville is about 60 miles north of Vermont. The city was largely populated by former slaves and their families. Dett's mother was born in Niagara Falls, Canada. His father, Robert Tue Dett and the rest of his ancestors that were born on the continent, were born in the United States. Dett's father had worked on the railroad but eventually bought a hotel in Niagara Falls, New York. Dett had two older brothers Samuel W. and Arthur Newton respectively. Arthur was shot in a childhood accident and died as a result. Dett had one sister, Harriet who died at the age of two. He began to show a lot of talent as a child. His first piano teacher was Mrs. Marshall. After the family moved to Niagara Falls, New York he began to study with John Weiss.

The first college that Dett attended was Niagara Falls Collegiate Institute. From there he went on to study at Halstead Conservatory in Lockport, new York. Dett also completed studies at Columbia University, Eastman College and Harvard Unversity. At Harvard he won the Bowdoin prize for his essay "Emancipation of Negro Music." Dett received his Doctorate in Music from Oberlin college.

In 1916 he married Helen Elise Smith. She was an accomplished pianist and had been the first Black to graduate from the Damrosch School of Musical Art. In 1921 this school was absorbed by the Juilliard School of Music. Two girls were born to this marriage Helen Charlotte and Josephine Elizabeth.

He taught at various colleges during the course of his career, Lane College in Jackson City, Mississippi, Lincoln Institute in Jefferson, Missouri and Hampton Institute, Hampton, Virginia. At Hampton he became the head of the Music Department. While at Hampton he edited the 1927 edition of "Religious Folk Songs of the Negro as Sung at Hampton Institute." It was during this time that he developed the Hampton Choir to such a level of professionalism that they were invited to perform in various concerts halls in Europe. Dett used these tours to help bring the tradition Afro-American Music to Europe. He also organized a musical art society at Hampton.

Dett won the Francis K. Boot prize for "Don't Be Weary Traveler. "

Indeed, Nathaniel Dett achieved a great deal of fame as a concert pianist and a composer during his lifetime. Many musicians will remember him for his two most famous piano works: "Magnolias" and "In the Bottoms." Most Black people will remember him for his choral arrangement of "Listen to The Lambs" which has helped to beautify so many Black church services.

Dett dedicated his life to making serious musicians respect the Afro-American Spiritual and give it its rightful place in the musical world.

Some of the firms that currently publish some of his works are:
"Listen to The Lambs" Publisher, G. Schirmer, New York City
"Collected piano works of R. Nathaniel Dett", Publisher Summy Birchard, Evanston, Illinois
Another firm that has published some of his works is Schmidt, Hall and McCreary in Minneapolis, Minnesota.

Dean Dixon

Dean Dixon
(Charles Rolston Dean Dixon)
January 10, 1915 - November 4, 1976
Conductor

Dean Dixon was born in New York City on 35th Street where Macy's now stands. His parents moved to Harlem when he was five months old and that's where he grew up. He was gifted with very high relative pitch. His parents were from the West Indies. His father, Henry Charles Dixon, is deceased. His mother, McClara Rolston Dixon, celebrated her 91st birthday in 1971. His father was a trained lawyer but had to work as a bellhop in this country. Even before he could walk, his mother carried him to concerts. At the age of five he could read music and had some degree of facility on the violin. Dean Dixon's first wife was the late Vivian Rivkin who was an American pianist. His second wife was Mary Mandelin, who is a Finnish Playwright. He has a daughter Diane from his first marriage and a daughter Nina, who was born July 28, 1954 from his second marriage. His widow is Roswith Blume, a German Journalist.

At 15 while attending Dewitt Clinton High School he founded his own music school, which bore his name. At 17 he organized his own chorus and orchestra for which he used his lunch money to buy the music. Upon graduation from high school Mr. Dixon auditioned for the Institute of Musical Art of the Juilliard School of Music (the undergraduate division) and was accepted. He auditioned on the violin. He majored in violin for half a year and then switched his major concentration to Music Pedagogy (Music Education). This enabled him to study 15 other instruments in addition to the violin, as well as, everything from keyboard harmony to the Dalcroze method of Eurythmics -- the art of moving harmoniously to improvised music. To complete this vast span of subjects Mr. Dixon also studied orchestral conducting with Adolph Schmid. In 1934 while attending Juilliard he made his violin debut at the YWCA on 137th street. Dean Dixon graduated from Juilliard in 1936 with a Bachelor of Science degree. Between 1936 and 1939 in addition to teaching he began studying conducting with Albert Stoessel on a fellowship at Juilliard. At the same time he began a Master of Arts in Music Education at Columbia University. He received his Master's from Columbia in 1939.

He made his Town Hall Debut in 1937 and conducted the League of Music Lovers Chamber Orchestra at this concert.

In 1938 he founded the New York Chamber Orchestra.

58

He conducted the music for "John Henry" by Roark Bradford and Jacques Wolfe in 1939. The show starred Paul Robeson. (See page 110).

In the summer of 1940 he conducted the New York City Symphony Orchestra. He gave a concert with the Dean Dixon Symphony Orchestra in lower Harlem at which Mrs. Eleanor Roosevelt was the guest of honor. Samuel Chotzinoff attended this concert and as a result invited him to conduct the NBC Symphony Orchestra. In 1941 he made his debut with the NBC Symphony Orchestra (also known as the Toscanini Symphony) and became the first Black conductor ever to conduct a major American Orchestra. In the summer of that same year he made his debut as conductor of the New York Philharmonic Symphony Orchestra. This gave him the distinction of being the first Black to ever conduct this organization. As he was only 26 years old at the time, in all probability he was the youngest conductor to conduct this organization. The program consisted of works by the masters as well as some works by a young Chinese Hawaiian named Daikeong Lee. Lee and Dixon had been schoolmates at Juilliard. He was also placed on the Honor Roll in Race Relations in 1941.

In January 1942 Mr. Dixon conducted the NBC Symphony Orchestra. In May of that year he conducted the New York Chamber Orchestra in a concert at Town Hall. He conducted the New York Philharmonic in July. At this performance he presented the American premiere of the "First Symphony" by Khatchaturian.

In 1943 he conducted the Philadelphia Orchestra.

He founded the American Youth Orchestra and guest conducted the Boston Symphony Orchestra in 1944.

In 1945 he began work on a Rosenwald Fellowship. During that same year he also received:
- The Newspaper Guild Page One Award
- The Lincoln Steffens Award "in recognition for outstanding musicianship and intense efforts for serious music, including the organization of an interracial youth orchestra."
- National Association for American Composers and conductors Award of Merit "for conspicuous work in the education of American Youth in Music."

59

In 1947 he completed his work on the Rosenwald Fellowship.

In 1948 he received the Urban League Certificate of Recognition Award for outstanding achievement. That same year he received the Alice M. Ditson Award from Columbia University for being the outstanding American Conductor of 1947-1948. He received $1000.00 as part of the award. As he wandered through his homeland he hoped that some major American Orchestra would give him a post as its permanent conductor. This dream was never fulfilled and in 1949 he left for Europe, a disappointed young Black Conductor.

He struggled for four years in France trying to make a living. During this time he guest conducted the National Radio Symphony of Paris. (1949)

In 1953 he became the permanent conductor of the Goteborg Orchestra in Sweden. During this time in Europe Mr. Dixon guest conducted all over Europe including Czechoslovakia, Amsterdam, Hamburg, Athens, Barcelona, Berlin, Brussels and Budapest to mention a few.

He became the permanent conductor of the Radio Frankfurt Symphony Orchestra in 1960. A few years later he became the permanent conductor of the Sydney Symphony in addition to his duties at Frankfurt. After a few years of flying between Europe and Sydney, Australia he decided it was too strenuous and resigned his Sydney post.

He returned to the U. S. in 1970 and was presented the keys to New York City by Mayor Lindsay. He guest conducted the New York Philharmonic.

In the 1971-1972 season he guest conducted: The Milwaukee Symphony, Detroit Symphony, National Symphony, The Prague Symphony Orchestra while it was in Philadelphia, and a Young People's concert with the New York Philharmonic. He also conducted a performance of the New York Symphony plus many European orchestras and other orchestras around the world.

In the 1972-1973 season he made his debut with the Chicago Symphony and conducted in Europe extensively.

During the 1973-1974 season he conducted throughout Europe and participated in the opening series of the New Sydney Opera House after having been away from Australia for seven years.

60

During the 1974-1975 season he returned to the Philadelphia Orchestra in addition to numerous other engagements.

He also conducted in Tokyo, Buenos Aires, Belgrad, Bern Copenhagen, Florenz, Israel, London, Melbourne, Mexico City, Milan, Monaco, Poland, and the list goes on ad infinitum.

His hobbies were: Cooking, Swimming, Ping Pong, Dancing and Jazz.

He taught at many institutions, including: the University of Wisconsin, Juilliard School of Music, Manhattan School of Music, Salzburg Morzarteum/ Austria, Jeunesses Musicales, Weikersheim/West Germany, Radio Hilversum/Holland.

He served as a Music Consultant for the New York City Kindergarten to 6B Teachers Association.

He created "Music for Millions Concerts," which were symphony concerts given free of charge, he inaugurated the "Hidden Curtain" radio auditions for discovery of new talents; and also innovated "Symphony at Midnight," concerts for people who are unable to get to concerts at regular hours.

He contributed articles to the many publications, including the Musical Courier, Music Educators' Journal, Music World Almanac, Music Publishers Journal.

He has been mentioned in the following books:
"Who's Who"
"The World Who's Who of Musicians"
"Riemann's Music Lexicon"
"Die Music in Geschicte and Gegenwart" by Barenreiter
"Dictionary of International Biography"
"The Ebony Success Library"
"Leaders of Black America"

He recorded for the following record companies:
American Recording Society
Ariola
Barenreiter
Musicaphon

61

Nonesuch Records
Supraphon
Westminster

He recorded the following composers:
Beethoven, Brahms, Cowell, Dvorak, Gershwin, Hanson, Haydn, Liszt,
Luening, Macdowell, Mason, Mendelssohn, Moore, Mozart, Piston, Powell,
Schubert, Schumann, Smetana, Sowerby, Swanson, Thompson,
Tchaikowsky, and Ward.

On November 7, 1976 I attended a concert by the Symphony of the New
World. It was there that I learned that Dean Dixon had died a few days
earlier. Although we had prepared this sketch by means of correspondence
I felt as though I had lost a dear friend. I sat down a few days later and
wrote an anthem in his memory. I will never forget the kind and
encouraging letters he sent to me.

Mattiwilda Dobbs

Mattiwilda Dobbs
Soprano

Mattiwilda Dobbs was the fifth daughter of six born to her family. It was decided that this fifth daughter should be named after her maternal grandmother Mattie Wilda. This was how Mattiwilda Dobbs received her given name. She was born in Atlanta, Georgia. Her father, John Wesley Dobbs was a railway mail clerk who became prominent in Masonic and civil-rights activities. Her mother, Irene Thompson Dobbs, was a housewife.

At the age of seven Miss Dobbs began to study the piano. She continued to study the piano for the next ten years. Her first performance as a singer was at the First Congregational Church in Atlanta.

At 17 she entered Spelman College in Atlanta and began her vocal studies under Naomi Maise and Willis James.

In 1946 she graduated from Spelman. She graduated as first in her class with majors in Music and Spanish. She left for New York that year where she began studying with Madame Lotte Leonard, who had been a famous Lieder and Oratorio singer in Germany. At the same time she began work on a Master's degree in Spanish at Columbia University.

In the summer of 1947 she attended the University of Mexico City and appeared as soloist in the University's annual festival of music. In the fall of that year she won a Marian Anderson Scholarship.

In 1948 she completed her Master of Arts degree at Columbia University and received a scholarship from the Mannes College of Music to attend its opera workshop.

In the summer of 1949 she received a scholarship to the opera workshop at the Berkshire Music Center, Tanglewood, Massachusetts.

In 1950 she went to Paris on a John Hay Whitney Opportunity Fellowship to study French Repertoire with Pierre Bernac and to Spain to study Spanish repertoire with Lola Rodriguez de Aragon.

In October 1951 she won first prize at the international music competition sponsored by the Conservatory of Music at Geneva. The prize for this competition was a performance with the Netherlands Orchestra. She won the prize and later that year she appeared with the Netherlands Orchestra in a performance of Stravinsky's "Le Rossignol" at the Holland Festival.

During the 1952-1953 season after having performed in the Scandinavian capitals, as well as, Belgium, Holland, France, Italy and England she made her debut at La Scala in Milano as Elvira in Rossini's "L'Italiana in Algeri." <u>She was the first Negro to sing in that house</u>. Later that same month at her La Scala Debut, she sang in the opera house at Genoa, Italy. She appeared as the Queen of the Night in "The Magic Flute" by Mozart.

In 1953 she appeared at the Glyndebourne festival in England. She appeared as Zervinetta in "Ariadne auf Naxos " by Richard Strauss. She was so successful in that role that she was also invited to appear at the Royal Opera House in Covent Garden that same season. At Covent Garden, England she appeared in the following roles: The Queen in "Coq d'or," Gilda in "Rigoletto," Lucia in "Lucia Di Lammermoor," Olymin in "The Tales of Hoffman," and the Forest Bird in Siegfried."

In March 1954 she made her New York debut as Zerbinetta with the Little Orchestra Society at Town Hall. She received a standing ovation and rave reviews from the critics. Later that season she made her first U. S. concert tour and appeared at the Edinburgh Festival in Scotland in a recital and an opera.

In the midst of an exciting career she met and married Win Rodriguez, a Spanish script writer. He died in 1954.

In June of 1954 Miss Dobbs was chosen to sing a command performance of "Coq d' or" before Queen Elizabeth II, Prince Phillip and the visiting King Gustav Adolf and late Queen Louise of Sweden at Covent Garden. King Gustav Adolf decorated Miss Dobbs with the Order of the North Star.

In the fall of 1954 in addition to performances at Covent Garden she sang recitals in: France, Belgium, Holland (The Netherlands) , Switzerland, and London.

In January 1955 she returned to the U.S. to perform a Town Hall Recital and her second U.S. concert tour. In March she performed again with The Little Orchestra Society and then left on a tour of the Caribbean, Mexico, and Central America.

For the next three months after this tour she did a series of 35 concerts in Australia. In October Miss Dobbs made her debut with the San Francisco Opera in "Coq d'or" by Rimsky Korsakov.

In 1956 she made her Metropolitan Opera debut as Gilda in "Rigoletto".

In 1957 she married Bengt Janzon who is a Swedish newspaper man and government and public relations employee. She made her home in Stockholm, Sweden.

She has performed often at the Royal Swedish Opera, The Oslo and Helsinki Operas and has performed many concerts on radio and television throughout all of Scandinavia. Also during the 1957 season she made a tour of Israel with the Israeli Philharmonic Orchestra.

In 1959 she toured Australia again and also New Zealand. She returned to Israel that same season for another concert tour with the Israeli Philharmonic. She spent six weeks of the season at the Bolshoi Opera in Russia as part of the U.S.-Soviet Union Cultural exchange program.

Between 1961 and 1963 Miss Dobbs made numerous appearances at the Hamburg Staats Oper and appeared in a new production of "Rigoletto" by the celebrated director Walter Felsenstein of the Comische Oper, Berlin. In addition to Gilda she has also appeared at the Comische Oper as Rosina in "The Barber of Seville" by Mozart; Konstanze in "Die Entfuhrung Aus Dem Serail"; Olympia in the "Tales of Hoffman" and the Forest Bird in "Siegfried".

In 1968 she made a "Third World" tour and sang in India, Thailand and New Zealand.

She has also performed at the Vienna State Opera and appeared at the Glyndebourne Opera on three other occasions, as well as, in a performance of "Die Zauberflote" as Queen of the Night.

She was a member of the Metropolitan Opera Company for eight years. In addition to the other roles we have already mentioned she has also sung Zerlina in "Don Giovanni" at the Metropolitan Opera House.

In addition to performances at the Met and concerts in Europe she also teaches. She is the Artist-in-residence at Spelman College. In August 1975 she also became a member of the staff of the University of Illinois in Champain-Urbana, Illinois and the University of Texas in Austin.

Her discography includes:

(Renaissance) "The Pearl Fishers" by Bizet
(Columbia) "German and French Songs" accompanied by Gerald Moore
(His Masters Voice)   "Die Entfuhrung Aus dem Serail" by Mozart (in English, conducted by Yehudi Menuhin. She sings the role of Konstanze)
----------------------"Don Giovanni" by Mozart
(Deutsche Grammophon)   "Tales of Hoffman" by Offenbach
(She sings Olympia and Antonia)
(Columbia) "Opera Arias and excerpts from 'Rigoletto'"

Roland Hayes
Picture courtesy Mrs. Theresa Lott Saunders.
Enlarged by James S. Gordon

Roland Hayes
June 3, 1887 - January 1, 1977
Tenor, Arranger

Roland Hayes was born in Little Row, Georgia. (The town had originally been named Curryville). His father's name was William Hayes. William Hayes was an ex-slave and his trade was carpentry. Roland Hayes' mother's name was Fannie Hayes. Fannie Hayes was the granddaughter of an African Chieftan named Aba Ougi. His slave-master gave him the name of Char when he brought him to this country. Aba Ougi had a son named Peter. Peter married a woman named Mand and to this marriage Fannie Hayes as well as three brothers: Robert, Wiltsie, and Simon and one other sister, Maria were born. Fannie Hayes was born a slave.

Roland Hayes had five brothers: William Jr. , Nathaniel, John, Robert, Jesse and one sister, Mattie.

The community that he grew up in was called Flatwoods. As a boy Roland Hayes began to sing with his church choir. His father died in 1898 when he was only 11. At this point he began to work as a farmhand. Later he went to work at the Evans Sash-weight Foundry in Chattanooga, Tennessee.

Roland Hayes was introduced to classical music by a professor Calhoun from Oberlin Conservatory.

In 1905 Mr. Hayes began his professional studies at Fisk University in Nashville, Tennessee. While at Fisk his sponsor was a Miss Robinson. During his attendance at Fisk University he was a member of the Fisk Jubilee Singers.

After he left Fisk he studied voice with Arthur J. Hubbard.

In 1912 he made his Concert Debut at Symphony Hall in Boston.

In 1914 Booker T. Washington asked him to sing duets with Harry T. Burleigh (see page 36) on his lecture tours.

69

In 1920 he met William Brennan who was the manager of the Boston Symphony Orchestra. He told Brennan of his hopes and Brennan told him that no one of the Black race would ever be accepted in the field of classical music. Later that same year he went to London and made his European concert Debut at Aeolian Hall in London. It was a success.

On April 21, 1921 he performed a concert at Wigmore Hall in England. As a result of that concert he was asked to sing before the King and Queen of England.

In 1922 he performed in France. During that same year he received an honorary Doctorate from Fisk University.

In 1923 he performed in Prague and Vienna.

By this time he had already become an established singer. He returned to the United States in 1923 and signed a contract with Walter Brennan and this was quite unusual because at the time there were no managers who would handle Black artists. This was definitely a change of heart on the part of Brennan. He performed 30 concerts in the United States that year and became the first Black to sing to integrated audiences in the south.

In 1924 he performed in Germany and received the Spingarn Medal from the NAACP.

In 1927 he sang in Denmark; Florence (for the exiled Queen of Greece); Russia and Amsterdam.

In 1930 and 1931 he toured Europe.

In 1932 he married his cousin Alzada Mann.

In 1933 he made his Town Hall Debut and his daughter, Afrika Fanzada, was born that same year.

In 1935 he sang at the dedication of the Theodore Roosevelt Memorial.

In 1940 he performed for the Library of Congress and at a festival held by the
Gertrude Whittall Foundation where he appeared with Dorothy Maynor.
(See page 104)

During World War II he performed for the allied troops at Royal Albert Hall in London. At this performance he performed with a 100-voice choir comprised entirely of soldiers.

In 1962 on the celebration of his 75th birthday Roland Hayes received an honorary scroll from Mayor Wagner of New York City.

He also performed at Tuskegee Institute in Alabama. He arranged many Afro-American Spirituals and performed many of his own arrangements. Roland Hayes gathered most of his arrangements into one book called "My Songs."

Roland Hayes was quite remarkable in several ways. An authority on Afro-American Spirituals in his own right, he was still concertizing right up until the time of his death, which was quite remarkable for a man in his age bracket. He was an artist of fine caliber and an excellent teacher.

Roland Hayes toured the United States for over 50 years. McKinley Helm has written Mr.Hayes' Biography entitled: "Angel Mo' and her Son Roland Hayes" published by Little, Brown and Company.

His daughter, Afrika Hayes is married and has two daughters. She is a concert artist and a Soprano. She has also served on several college faculties. She has taught at Virginia State College, North Carolina State College, and the New England Conservatory. She is teaching at Brimmer and May, which is a private school for girls. Miss Hayes concertizes by her maiden name. Both of her daughters are musical and are studying ballet.

Roland Hayes recordings include:
(Vanguard) " Life of Christ in Folksongs"
(Veritas-Columbia) "Roland Hayes in a Program of Spirituals and Art Songs" (Vanguard) " Six Centuries of Song"

71

Dr. Hall Johnson
Picture courtesy Mrs. Alice Johnson Foster

Dr. Hall Johnson
March 12,1888 - April 30, 1970
Arranger, Composer, Conductor, Violinist and Violist

Dr. Hall Johnson was born in Athens, Georgia; His father was William D. Johnson, A.M., D.D., PhD., bishop of the A.M.E. Church. His mother was Alice Sansom Johnson, an early student of Atlanta University, Atlanta, Georgia.

As a child Hall Johnson was taught piano by an older sister, Mary Elizabeth, and his father taught him Solfeggio, the 6 tone scale used in sacred music by the ancients.

The most fascinating experiences during his childhood were listening daily to the clear soprano singing by his maternal grandmother, of various songs of Negro origin and listening to the singing of a number of ex-slaves as they walked through his neighborhood. He was also fascinated by the beautiful singing that he heard at revivals.

Hall Johnson began his early studies at Knox Institute in Athens, Georgia. He later attended Atlanta University. From there he went to Allen University in Columbia, South Carolina.

In 1907 after having studied violin alone for three years he went to Philadelphia. There he entered the Hahn School of Music and continued his violin studies.

Sometime prior to 1910 he wrote a prize-winning composition. As a result of this composition he was accepted as a Theory and Composition student at the University of Pennsylvania in 1910. He studied composition privately with Percy Goetchius and eventually went to New York City to study composition there.

In 1914 he joined the personal orchestra of Mr. and Mrs. Vernan Castle in New York.

During the 1925-1926 season he played with the orchestra of "Shuffle Along", which was an all-Negro revue. He later played with the orchestra of "Running Wild" which was another very successful all Negro show.

73

In 1925 he organized the Hall Johnson Choir, which was dedicated to the art of preserving the Afro-American Spiritual. Later in 1925 he arranged and conducted the music for the original "Green Pastures" for which his choir supplied the music.
In 1933 he wrote the book and music for "Run Li'l Chillun," which was a Black music drama.

In 1934 he received an Honorary Doctorate Degree from the Philadelphia Music Academy.
In 1941 he went to Los Angeles where he organized the "Festival Negro Chorus" to supply scholarships for young Black Musicians.

In 1946 he organized the "Festival Negro Chorus" of New York City. Later in 1946 he presented an original cantata "Son of Man" at the New York City Center.

In 1951 the Hall Johnson Choir represented the State Department at the International Festival of Fine Arts in Berlin.

The Hall Johnson Choir was very successful. So much so that they received invitations to various countries and cities around the world. During this time the choir toured Germany and performed in Vienna, Austria.

From 1952 to 1957 Dr. Johnson performed with various choirs in and around the Los Angeles area.

In 1957 he returned to New York City and reorganized The Hall Johnson Choir and began working with Belafonte Enterprises.

Dr. Johnson was one of the few Black composers to combine the melodies of the Spirituals with orchestral writing.

Dr. Johnson received many citations and awards during his lifetime. In 1962 he received a citation for "35 years of cultural contributions to the world," signed by Robert F. Wagner, Mayor of New York City.

In 1970 he was awarded the George Frederic Handel Award (The highest award the city can offer) by John V. Lindsay, Mayor of New York City.

Dr. Johnson was concerned about the state of the Afro-American Spiritual. And the main ambition of his life was to preserve Afro-American Spirituals in their purity. To this end he dedicated his life.

Musicians like this will have lived in vain unless more Black musicians of today do something to help preserve this art form.

Some of our other well known arrangers and conductors such as Jester Hairston and Leonard DePaur (see page 55) studied orchestration and the interpretation of American Spirituals with Dr. Hall Johnson.

Some of his best-known choral arrangements are:

"I've Been Buked" (publisher, G. Schirmer, New York City)
"When I Was Sinkint Down" (G. Schirmer,N.Y.C.)
"Thirty Negro Spirituals Arranged for Voice and Piano" (G. Schirmer)

Another very popular piece of his is "Ain't Got Time to Die". This is actually an original composition written in the style of a Afro-American spiritual. There are upwards of another 50 of his arrangements of spirituals in print. At the time of his death there were other arrangements, which were not in print. The Robbins Music Company of New York City also carries some of his arrangements.

John Rosamond Johnson seated at the piano, **James Weldon Johnson** standing

James Weldon Johnson
June 17,1871-1938
Arranger, Librettist, Poet, Writer

James Weldon Johnson was born in Jacksonville, Florida. Compared to most people of his time whose family had the experience of slavery, quite a lot is known about James Weldon Johnson's lineage.

One of his maternal great-grandmothers was an African woman whose slave name was Sarah. Her husband was a Captain Symonett. Sarah and Captain Symonett had nine children. One of these nine children was a daughter named Mary Symonett. Mary Symonett married Stephen Dillet. Stephen Dillet's mother was a Haitian woman named Hester Argo. His father had been a French officer named Etienne Dillet who was stationed in Haiti. Stephen Dillet was born approximately 1796. His first occupation had been a tailor. He later entered politics and became a very successful politician. Helen Louise Dillet, the child of Mary Symonett and Stephen Dillet, was born on August 4,1842 in Nassau in the Bahamas.

Helen Louise Dillet married James Johnson and the offspring of this marriage were: Marie Louise, July 10, 1868-1870, James Weldon, and John Rosamond, born August 11, 1873. (See next sketch) About 1876 the Johnson family adopted a girl, Agnes Marion Edwards, who was already in her teens.

James Weldon Johnson's mother, Helen Louise Dillet Johnson, had received a good education and was an excellent singer. Although she was not professionally trained, she sang well enough to give concerts. James Johnson was present at one of these concerts. It was at this concert that James Weldon Johnson's parents met for the first time. She was the first colored woman to become a public school teacher in Florida.

James Johnson was a free man born in Richmond, Virginia on August 26, 1830. His first occupation had been that of a headwaiter. A self-taught man, James Johnson later became a minister at one of the large Churches in Fernandina, Florida.

The first instrument that James Weldon Johnson studied was the organ. His mother was his first organ teacher. When he was almost seven his family got rid of the organ and purchased a piano. At this point his mother began to give him piano lessons. Later he studied piano with a Frenchman whose name I was not able to uncover. James Weldon Johnson also studied the fundamentals of violin. Additionally, his father played the guitar as a hobby and later gave him some lessons in the fundamentals of playing the guitar.

J. W. Johnson attended the Stanton School for Colored Children. This was the only grammar school for colored children in Jacksonville at that time. His mother had already become a teacher at the Stanton School by the time he was old enough to attend school.

In 1887 he started his high school studies in the preparatory division of Atlanta University. He went on to complete his undergraduate work at Atlanta University, where he majored in English. He had learned Spanish, while still quite young from conversing with a Cuban boy who had come to live with him and his family. By the time he entered the preparatory division of Atlanta University he was already fluent in Spanish.

While attending Atlanta University, James Weldon Johnson found little time to study piano. He did try to keep up with his knowledge of the guitar. In order to utilize this talent he sang bass in a college quartet and played guitar to accompany them.

After graduating From Atlanta University, J. W. Johnson returned to Jacksonville and eventually became principal of the Stanton School for Colored Children. Under his leadership the Stanton School was expanded from a grammar school to a school encompassing grades one through twelve.

While principal of the Stanton School, in 1900 James Weldon Johnson wrote the words to "Lift Every Voice and Sing" for a celebration to commemorate Lincoln's Birthday. His brother, John Rosamond Johnson, wrote the music for the song. The children sang the song at the program. The song was later adopted by the National Association for the Advancement of Colored People "NAACP "as its National Anthem and there-by became the Black National Anthem in this country.

He set up the Daily American, which was the first colored daily newspaper.

He studied law privately with a Mr. Ledwith. He took an open courtroom bar examination and became the first Black to be admitted to the bar through an open examination in the state of Florida. After being admitted to the bar he helped to prepare a friend for the bar examination. After his friend passed the bar they set up a law partnership.

He moved to New York where he and his brother set up a music writing partnership. They began to write musicals and showtunes for use in musicals written by other musicians. Occasionally he would write lyrics for other musicians and his brother would write music for other lyricists. (See list at end of sketch). He began to take graduate courses at Columbia University in English and writing.

The team that he and his brother set up was eventually joined by Robert Cole, an actor, singer and composer.

About 1906 the team of Cole and the Johnson Brothers broke up. Robert Cole and John Rosamond Johnson started to go on the road as a vaudeville act while James Weldon Johnson was appointed to the position of consul at Puerto Cabello, Venezuela.

In 1909 he was assigned the position of Consul to Corinto, Nicaragua.

In 1910 he married Grace Nail.

In 1913 he resigned from the United States Consular service. At this time he wrote some scenarios for some movies. (see glossary)

In 1914 he became contributing editor for the New York Age and helped to organize the American Society of Composers, Authors and Publishers (ASCAP).

In 1915 he translated the Opera "Goyescas" from Spanish into English for its first performance at the Metropolitan Opera House.

In 1916 he became field secretary of the National Association for the Advancement of Colored People (NAACP). He served as field secretary for 14 years and made a reputation as an organizer, civil rights worker and lobbyist. He helped to establish many new branches for the organization.

In 1925 he and his brother wrote a collection of spirituals called, "The book of American Negro Spirituals" (Viking Press).

He also received the Spingarn Medal from the NAACP, and the Harmon Award for his collection of poems entitled "God's Trombones."

In 1926 he and his brother published a second collection of Negro spirituals.

James Weldon Johnson was elected to the Board of Trustees of Atlanta University and helped to merge Morehouse College, Spelman College and Atlanta University to form the Greater Atlanta University.

He received honorary Doctor of Literature Degrees from Howard University and Talladega College.

In 1930 he published "Black Manhattan," a history of Black stage performances in New York from the African Company of 1826 to the first performance of "Green Pastures" in 1930. It was the first book of its kind.

He spent part of his career teaching in the Creative Literature department of Fisk University. In 1933 he published his own biography "Along This Way" (Viking Press, New York).

James Weldon Johnson was an artist in the truest sense of the word. Some of his best known works are: "The Creation," which was a poem from the collection "God's Trombones," his controversial novel "The Biography of an Ex-Colored Man" and his words for the Black National Anthem, "Lift Every Voice and Sing."

A partial list of some of his other works follows:
Compositions by J.W. Johnson and J.R. Johnson
Since You Went Away (Song)
Lift Every Voice and Sing (Black National Anthem)
Louisiana Lize (song)
Toloso (Opera)
Art Songs

Compositions by Cole and Johnson Brothers
Humpty Dumpty (Musical)
In Newport (Musical) Pub. Klaw and Erlanger

80

The Maiden with the Dreamy Eyes (song) Pub. Joseph W. Stern co.
Mandy Won't You Let Me Be Your Beau (Song) "   "
Nobody's Lookin' But The Owl and The Moon (song)"   "
Tell Me Dusky Maiden   (song)   "   "
The Old Flag Never Touched the Ground (song)   "   "
My Castle On The Nile   (song)   "   "
Under The Bamboo Tree   (song)   "   "
Oh Didn't He Ramble   (song)   "   "
Congo Love Song   (song)   "   "

Run Brudder Possum (song)   Pub. Rogers Brothers
Come Out,Dinah, On The Green   "   "

Musicals the above trio had songs in
Sleeping Beauty
The Supper Club
Belle of Bridgeport
Champagne Charlie
Lazy Moon

Compositions by J.W. Johnson with musicians other than the above

A Broadway Show with Jerome Kern (I could not find the name of the show)
Art Songs with Harry T. Burleigh (See page 36)
Cannibal King with Will Marion Cook

The Galaxy Music Corporation also publishes one of his compositions
(Galaxy Music Corp., N.Y.C.)

John Rosamond Johnson
August 11, 1873 - November 11, 1954
Composer, Arranger, Pianist, Bass

John Rosamond Johnson was born in Jacksonville, Florida. His father, James Johnson was born in Richmond, Virginia. (See previous sketch for further information.

John Rosamond Johnson's mother, Helen Louise Billet Johnson was born in Nassau in the Bahamas on August 4, 1842. Mrs. Johnson was a schoolteacher at the Stanton School for Colored Children. She was also considered an amateur writer. (For further information see previous sketch.)

John Rosamond Johnson had one sister, Mary Louise, who died at the age of two. He had one older brother, James Weldon, born June 17, 1871 (see previous sketch). His parents later adopted Agnes Marion Edwards.

John Rosamond Johnson attended the Stanton School for Colored Children, where his mother was one of the teachers. It was here that he obtained his grammar school education.

J. R. Johnson's mother was his first organ and piano teacher.

In 1890 he entered the New England Conservatory in Boston. I was not able to ascertain exactly which degree he earned while he was there. He left the New England Conservatory in 1896. While studying at the New England Conservatory he had two original compositions published.

From 1896 to 1897 he traveled with various musical shows. Among them were: "A Creole Show" (a musical comedy); "The Octoroons;" and "Oriental America."

In 1897 he set to music a poem that his brother had written about Easter. This composition took the form of an anthem. He returned to Jacksonville later that year and became the choirmaster and organist for one of the large Baptist churches there. He also began to teach at the Baptist Academy there once a week and set up a private studio.

82

In 1898 John R. Johnson wrote a small operetta for which his brother supplied the lyrics; this operetta was from the music of "Geisha" and "Runaway Girl."

In 1899 he and his brother collaborated on the opera "Toloso." As was their custom he wrote the music and his brother wrote the lyrics. The opera satirized American Imperialism (e.g., the annexation of Texas and the Spanish American War). During the summer of 1899 the Johnson brothers left for New York City to try and sell their opera. They were unable to get anyone to produce "Toloso" however they managed to meet many important people in the theater world, including several publishers. Before they left New York that summer they met Robert Cole, who was a talented actor and vaudeville singer. At the end of the summer they returned to their teaching positions in Jacksonville.

In 1900 James Weldon Johnson was invited to speak at a celebration commemorating Lincoln's Birthday. He decided to write a poem about Lincoln. That poem did not materialize. What did materialize was a poem depicting the struggles of Black people in this country. John Rosamond Johnson set this poem to music and it was sung by a chorus of 500 school children at the celebration. This song was later adopted by the NAACP as its national anthem and thereby became the National Anthem of Black people in this country. That song is "Lift Ev'ry Voice and Sing."

The Johnson Brothers later returned to New York and set up a music writing team with Robert Cole. J.R. Johnson wrote the music, J.W. Johnson wrote the lyrics and Robert Cole suggested changes and other ideas to improve both. By this time Robert Cole had already composed several songs of his own. (See previous sketch for a partial listing of their compositions).

At this point the Johnson brothers careers took different directions. James Weldon began to work as a Consul for the U.S. Government. John R. formed a team with Robert Cole. The team wrote musicals and became a vaudeville duo. John R. Johnson and Robert Cole began to tour the U. S. as a vaudeville team. They eventually toured London. John R. Johnson sang bass and played the piano for the vaudeville team.

In 1911 Robert Cole and J. R. Johnson made a tour of the United States with a show they had written entitled "The Shoo-Fly Regiment." The show had 60 people in it. Because of the racial barrier Black performers could not perform in first class theaters. Because of this situation they had to play in smaller houses for less money. Their managers, realizing that they were losing money, pulled out on them and left them to fend for themselves. J.R. Johnson and Cole had to use their own money to keep the company together and get back to New York.

In 1912 they made a tour of the United States with a show they had written called "Red Moon." This show also had some financial problems because of the racial barriers already mentioned. J.R. Johnson and Cole decided that it would be easier for them to return to the vaudeville stage as a duo. They found a manager who agreed to pay them $750.00 a week as a duet.

Very shortly thereafter Robert Cole died in a swimming accident.

John R. Johnson went to London and took a post as Director of Music at the Hammerstein Opera House. His father also died that year (1912 at the age of 82), and he went back to Jacksonville for the funeral.

While in Jacksonville he became engaged to Nora Floyd. She had been one of his piano pupils. He returned to London and sent for his fiancé. They were married in London in 1912. I was not able to ascertain how many children were born to this marriage. I do know that there was at least one daughter born to this marriage.

In 1918 he became Director of the New York Music School Settlement for Colored People. This school was located on 130th Street between Lenox and Seventh Avenues. We must remember that Harlem was at one time a predominantly White area and that during the early 1900's Blacks began to move into the area en masse.

John R. Johnson also spent part of his career teaching at Fisk University in Tennessee.

J. R. Johnson and his brother were some of the first famous Black musical writers who helped to break down many of the barriers that had been standing in the way of many of the Black musical writers before them. They made it easier for the Black musical writers who came after them.

84

But John Rosamond Johnson will best be remembered as the Black composer who wrote the music for the Black National Anthem.

Among the songs that J.R. Johnson wrote with someone other than his brother are:
"When the Colored Band Comes Marchin' Down the Street"
"Lil Gal" (The lyrics for both these songs were written by Paul Lawrence Dunbar.)

(Please see previous sketch for names of other compositions and a partial listing of his publishers).

He also collaborated with Harry B. Smith on several songs. Harry B. Smith was a prominent Black Librettist of the early 1900's.

(See previous sketch for picture of John Rosamond Johnson)

Henry Lewis

Henry Lewis
October 16, 1932 - January 26, 1996
Conductor, Double Bassist

Henry Lewis was born in Los Angeles. His father was a real estate salesman. At the age of five he began to study piano. At age six he began to study the Double Bass Violin. By the time he entered Junior High School he had already begun to conduct. Because of his desire to conduct he had begun to study most of the orchestral instruments. In the meantime he had become so proficient on his Double Bass that he had begun to give solo recitals. At 16 years after hearing one of Henry Lewis' solo recital, Henry Lewis was invited by Alfred Wallenstein to become a member of the Los Angeles Philharmonic. With this Henry Lewis achieved a number of notable accomplishments: the first Black to play with the Los Angeles Philharmonic; one of the few Blacks to become a regular member of a major American orchestra, and the youngest member of a major American orchestra. Upon graduation from high school he received a scholarship to the University of Southern California where he completed his undergraduate studies.

In 1951 he met a young Mezzo-Soprano named Marilyn Horne and a courtship began.

Drafted into the army in 1955, Henry Lewis became the conductor of the Seventh Army Symphony Orchestra. As the conductor of the Seventh Army Symphony Orchestra he toured Germany, the Netherlands and many more European Countries. He conducted over 150 concerts and recorded 52 concerts for broadcast over the U.S. Armed Forces station and the German Radio.

In 1957 upon release from the armed service, he resumed his post with the Los Angeles Philharmonic. In addition he began to work with a chamber opera group and taking voice lessons.

In 1960 Mr. Lewis founded the Los Angeles Chamber Orchestra. Later that same year he married the young mezzo-soprano he had been courting for nine years.

87

In 1961 Igor Markevitch, the maestro, became ill. A replacement had to be found for him. He had been scheduled to conduct two concerts with the Los Angeles Philharmonic Orchestra. Mr. Lewis was asked to conduct the two L.A. Philharmonic concerts, thereby making him one of the few Blacks who have conducted a major U.S. Orchestra. (Dean Dixon was the first, see page 66.) He became the first Black to conduct the Los Angeles Philharmonic and the first resident of Los Angeles to conduct the Los Angeles Philharmonic. Later that year he made his New York Debut with his Chamber Orchestra in the Washington Square Summer Chamber Orchestra Concerts. In 1963 he toured Europe with his chamber orchestra under the sponsorship of the State Department.

In 1965 he made his La Scala debut conducting "Gershwinana" which is a ballet-cantata based on George Gershwin's music.

In 1966 he made his Carnegie Hall debut as the Conductor of the American Opera Company in a performance of "Anna Bolena" by Donizetti.

In 1968 Mr. Lewis was named the permanent conductor of the New Jersey Symphony Orchestra, which has its home base in Newark, New Jersey. He became the first Black to be appointed the permanent conductor of a major American orchestra. (Dean Dixon dreamed of this honor years ago. I had hoped that Dean Dixon's desire for an American appointment would have been fulfilled.)

On October 16, 1972 Henry Lewis made his Metropolitan Opera Debut conducting "La Boheme." This made him the first Black conductor to conduct the Metropolitan Opera Company.

During the 1972-1973 season he also made his New York Philharmonic debut. The concluding composition on the program was the "1812 Overture" by Tchaikovsky complete with cannon shots and fireworks.

Mr. Lewis also conducted the New Jersey Symphony in its first series at Carnegie Hall during the 1972-1973 season.

He also conducted the following opera companies: Vancouver Opera Company, San Francisco Opera Company, the Los Angeles Opera Company, the Opera Company of Boston and the Montreal Opera Company.

He also conducted the following orchestras: the Chicago Symphony, San Francisco Symphony, Boston Symphony Orchestra, Cincinnati Symphony, American Symphony, Buffalo Symphony, Detroit Symphony, Baltimore Symphony, London Symphony, Royal Philharmonic and the RAI.

His wife is now a regular member of the Metropolitan Opera company. They are now separated and have a little daughter named Angela.

His discography includes:
(London)   "Bach and Handel Arias" Marilyn Horne Mezzo-Soprano
            "   "Carmen" by Bizet (excerpts)
"   "Don Jaun" by R. Strauss
"   "Mahler- Wagner Album" Marilyn Horne, Mezzo-Soprano
"   "Pathetique" Tchaikovsky
"   "Pastoral"- Beethoven
"   "Presenting Marilyn Horne"
"   "Rossini Arias" Marilyn Horne Mezzo-Soprano
"   "Souvenir of a Golden Era" Marilyn Horn Mezzo-Soprano.
"   " Til Eulenspigel" - R. Strauss

89

Robert McFerrin as Valentin
Picture courtesy Metropolitan Archives. Sedge LeBlang, photographer

Robert McFerrin
March 19, 1921 - November 24, 2006
Baritone

Robert McFerrin was born in Memphis, Tennessee. His father, Melvin McFerrin, was a minister. His mother's name is Mary McFerrin. Mr. McFerrin was born into a family of eight children, three brothers and five sisters. I was only able to ascertain the name of one brother, Meloin McFerrin. In 1936 his family moved to St. Louis, Missouri, where he attended Sumner High School and was first discovered by Wirt Watson. Mr. Watson later became one of his benefactors.

He began his professional study at Fisk University in Nashville, Tennessee, where he stayed for one year. From there he went to the Chicago College of Music.

In 1942 he entered the Army. He was released from the Army in 1946 at which time he re-entered the Chicago College of Music on a scholarship. When his scholarship expired he went home to St. Louis for a year. He worked and saved money to go back to Chicago. He received help from Mrs. Kriegsberger, who was the organist of Temple Israel. As fate worked out, he came to New York instead of going back to Chicago. He received a scholarship from Boris Goldovsky to Tanglewood.

Upon his return to New York he began to sing at the St. Marks Methodist Church. There he met and married Sarah Copper, who is also a singer. Mrs. McFerrin is a graduate of Howard University and has sung in Canada and the Caribbean. They now have two children, Robert Jr. and Brenda Joy. Robert Junior is a grammy winning conductor and vocalist.

In 1950 he sang with the New England Opera Company, Later that year he made his Town Hall Debut. In 1955 he began to study in the voice course of the Metropolitan Opera Company known as the Kathryn Long course. He was the first Black to be trained at the Met. Mr. McFerrin was the first Black man but the second Black person to sing at the Metropolitan Opera House. He was the first Black singer to become a regular member of the Metropolitan Opera company. His mother was 70 years old at the time of his Metropolitan Opera debut.

Mr. McFerrin has sung in Iceland, and at the World's Fair when it was in Brussels. He has sung in South America. He sang in the Broadway revival of "Green Pastures." One of his teachers was Ignaz Zitomirsky.

He was on the faculty of the St. Louis Conservatory. This baritone stands 5 feet, 6 inches tall.

Robert McFerrin's discography includes:

"Highlights of Rigoletto"

Dorothy Maynor

Dorothy Maynor
September 3, 1910 - February 19, 1996
Soprano

Dorothy Maynor was born in Norfolk, Virginia. She was born Dorothy Mainor. The spelling of her last name was changed when she began her singing career.

Her father, John Mainor, was a Methodist minister. Her mother was Alice Jeffries Mainor. Miss Maynor started singing in the choir at her father's church when she was still quite young.

She decided to become a home economics teacher and at 14 years of age entered Hampton Institute, which at that time offered high school and college level work. Music was her chief extracurricular activity but she still had not decided to make it her career.

In 1929 she joined the Hampton Choir under R. Nathaniel Dett (see page 24) and toured Europe. Dett realizing Miss Maynor's talent suggested to her that she study voice.

In 1933 she graduated from Hampton with a B.S. in Home Economics. While at Hampton, she was a scholarship student for four years. During these four years, she also played tennis and became president of the student government league. While there she also studied art, drama and dance.

In 1933 she sang for Dr. John Finley Williamson, who was the President of Westminster Choir College and received a scholarship. In 1935 she received an Mus. B. Degree in Choir Direction from Westminster Choir College, which is located in Princeton, New Jersey.

In the summer of 1935 she toured New England as soloist of the Hampton Choir. This time, after encouragement from some ladies who later became her patrons, she decided to study music as a career. Later that year she came to New York and studied voice with Wilfred Klaroth.

In 1936 to help cover expenses she worked as a musical director at a church in Brooklyn and taught at Hampton Institute.

94

In 1939 in between rehearsals at the Berkshire Festival in Lenox Massachusetts, Miss Maynor sang for Serge Koussevitsky, the conductor of the Boston Symphony Orchestra. This Festival is held in Lenox, Massachusetts. After singing at a picnic held for the Boston Symphony, the next day she was engaged to make recordings with the Boston Symphony. Later that year she made her Town Hall debut. This was such a success that she received immediate bookings. She was judged the outstanding performer and received the Town Hall Endowment Series Award. With this Award went an "Expense free" appearance at Town Hall.

During her first concert season, she toured the major cities of the United States and appeared as soloist with the New York Philharmonic, Boston Symphony, Philadelphia Orchestra and the Chicago Symphony.

She became the first Black person to do a series of concerts commemorating the 75th Anniversary of the Emancipating 13th Amendment to the Constitution. As a result of one of these concerts, she became the first Black to sing in Coolidge Auditorium in the Library of Congress.

She made her Carnegie Hall debut in 1941.

In 1942 while singing at the Municipal Building in Long Beach, California, a blackout occurred. 4,000 remained spellbound as they listened to her in total darkness.

She was soloist at the 50th Anniversary of the World Y.M.C.A., which took place at the Washington Cathedral in 1944. She was the first woman allowed to sing in the chancel.

In 1945 she was invited to be Director of Music at Bennett College in Greensboro, North Carolina. She did not accept this post but continued to study.

She made her South American debut in 1947.

In 1948 she sang at President Truman's inauguration.

She returned to Europe as a concert artist in 1949. Later that year she appeared as the first guest soloist in the N.B. C. concert series of 1949.

95

In 1950 she sang at the Watergate concerts in Washington, D.C. and on this occasion received the sesquicentennial (15oth) Memorial Medal authorized by Congress.

She sang at Constitution Hall, Washington, D.C. in 1951 and became the first Black artist to perform there. Marian Anderson had been denied use of the Hall prior to 1939 by the Daughters of the American Revolution, who owned the hall.

She is the wife of Rev. Shelby Albright Rooks, who is the pastor of St. James Presbyterian Church, where she is now Choir Director. She is the Director of the Harlem School of the Arts. In 1976 the federal Government gave her a very large grant to help develop the Harlem School of the Arts.

Rev. Rooks was Professor of Religion at Lincoln University in Pennsylvania when they met and married in 1942. Miss Maynor also maintains a small studio at Carnegie Hall. She has a small home on the York River in Virginia, which in her own words is, "A place to go to isolate yourself. A few boats on the river, a few bunnies on the lawn." She also likes fishing, tennis and "all kinds of housework."

In May of 1975 she was appointed to the Board of Directors of the Metropolitan Opera Association. She is the first Black to have this distinction.

Her recordings include:

"The Art of Dorothy Maynor" (RCA)

JOHN MOTLEY

Picture courtesy Mt. Olivet Baptist Church

John Motley
September 19, 1921 – May 27, 2011
Conductor, Pianist

John Motley was born in Cheraw, South Carolina. His father and mother's names were Frank and Sarah Davis Motley. Mr. Motley had two brothers and one sister. The four of them sang hymns together as children.

Mr. Motley did his undergraduate work at South Carolina State College where he majored in agriculture. Upon graduation from South Carolina State in 1941, he entered the Army. While in the Army he played piano and baritone horn in the 92nd Division Band. His division was known as the Buffalo Division.

Upon release from the Army he began to play with a dance band. He later entered New York University where he completed a Bachelor of Music and a Master of Music. While attending New York University he began to work as Director of Music at Janes United Methodist Church in Brooklyn, and to conduct the New York City Board of Education Community Chorus.

He has taught at Alexander Hamilton High School and Macon Junior High School 51. He founded the New York City All-City Junior High School Chorus.

When Marian Anderson went on her farewell tour Mr. Motley was her accompanist. (See page 14).

(See page 14).

In 1970 he became Assistant Director of Music for the New York City Board of Education as well as Director of the All-City High School Chorus. He is the first Black to hold these positions. In 1974 he was promoted to the rank of Acting Director of Music for the New York City Board of Education. He is the first Black to hold this position. He has also done graduate Work at Westminster Choir College in Princeton, New Jersey.

In addition to his duties at the Board of Education he is presently lecturing and giving voice instruction at the Manhattan School of Music and Teacher's College Columbia University. He is also Director of Music at Grace Congregational Church in Manhattan.

He has two sons: John Jr. and Michael.

98

Paul Robeson
Picture courtesy Paul Robeson Archives

Paul Robeson
April 9, 1898 - January 23, 1976
Bass-Baritone

Paul Robeson's father, Reverend William Drew Robeson was born in 1845 in Martin County, North Carolina. He was born a slave and escaped to the north in 1860 by means of the Underground Railroad. He worked his way through Lincoln University and became a minister. Rev. Robeson had two brothers Benjamin and John. He died in 1918.

Paul Robeson's mother was Maria Louisa Bustill Robeson. She was born November 8, 1853 in Philadelphia. She was a schoolteacher, who died in 1904 when the house accidentally caught on fire.

Paul Robeson was born in Princeton, New Jersey. At the time of his birth there were four other children living: William Drew Robeson Jr., 17; Reeve, l2; Benjamin, 6; and Marian his only sister, who was 4.

He did undergraduate work at Rutgers University, Brunswick, New Jersey, where he played football and won 4 athletic letters. He also won a total of nine athletic letters in three other sports: Baseball, Track and Basketball. In 1918 he was chosen All-American End by Walter Camp. He was a brilliant student and received the highest marks that had ever been earned at Rutgers since its founding in 1766. During his junior year at Rutgers he made Phi Beta Kappa.

Upon completion of his Degree at Rutgers, Mr. Robeson entered Columbia Law School from which he graduated in 1923.

While Robeson was in law school his career began to change. It was at this time that he met and married Eslanda Cardoza Goode. It was his wife who encouraged him to use his acting and singing abilities. His oldest brother William had discovered his singing voice some years earlier and had suggested that he study music. At that time singing was the farthest thing from Paul Robeson's mind.

In the course of his law studies his wife convinced him to take part in an amateur production of "Simon the Cyrenian" at the YMCA. Mr. Robeson took the part to please his wife. This role attracted the attention of some broadway producers and made his first professional appearance in "Voodoo."

100

Upon graduation from law school he took a position with a law firm. After meeting James Light and Eugene O'Neal from the Provincetown Theater he began to work with some professional acting companies.

In 1925 he gave his first U.S. Concert performance.

He toured Europe in 1926 and 1928.

In 1929 Robeson returned to the U.S. in triumph and made a concert tour.

He returned to Europe in 1931 and made another concert tour.

In 1936 he toured the Soviet Union.

He toured Europe again in 1938.

In 1945 he received an honorary Doctorate of Humane Letters from Morehouse College and the Spingarn Medal from the NAACP.

From 1950 to 1958 Paul Robeson was denied the right to travel anywhere outside the continental United States including, Canada, Mexico and Hawaii. His passport was revoked. This was a high price to pay for speaking one's mind.

He suffered a serious illness in 1961 and was forced to retire from the stage. At the beginning of his illness he was still in Europe. He returned to the U.S. three years later in 1964 and remained here until his death in 1976.

Among some of the dramatic roles he played were: "Emperor Jones", Crown in "Porgy and Bess," and "Othello."

He has written a combination essay and autobiography entitled "Here I Stand."

His son, Paul Robeson Jr., is in charge of the Paul Robeson Archives here in New York City.

Mr. Robeson continued to give encouragement to his people even after he retired from the stage.

His recordings include:
"Ballad for Americans"   (Vanguard)
"Robeson"   (Vanguard)
"Songs of Free Men and Spirituals"   (Odyssey)
"Paul Robeson in Live Performance"   (CCBG - Columbia)

Noah Francis Ryder
Picture courtesy Mrs. Noah Francis Ryder

Noah Francis Ryder
April 10, 1914 - April 17, 1964
Composer, Arranger, Conductor, Pianist

Noah Francis Ryder was born in Nashville, Tennessee. He was the son of Noah Walker Ryder, who was a musician. N.W. Ryder worked at Fisk University in the capacity of Singer and Teacher. N.W. Ryder's father had been a minister in the Methodist Church. Noah Walker Ryder also conducted the choir at the Mt. Zion Church in Cincinnati, Ohio.

Noah Francis Ryder's mother was Lillian Beasley Ryder, who died when he was three. His father remarried and his second wife, who is still living, is Olive Love Ryder. Olive Love Ryder was formerly the registrar at Kentucky State College and is a retired schoolteacher from the public schools of Cincinnati.

Noah Francis Ryder had one brother, Walker Ware Ryder and one sister, Jane Ryder. Jane Ryder died in 1969.

N.F. Ryder grew up in Cincinnati where he attended the Walnut Hills High School and played in the school's symphonic band. It was during this time he began to compose.

In 1931 he entered Hampton Institute. While there a period of great creativity began. It was at this time that he began to come to the public's attention. The Hampton Choir, Hampton Trade School Singers, and the Royal Hamptonians, all began to perform his compositions. The Royal Hamptonians was a Jazz Band he led. He also formed the internationally known "Deep River Boys" during this period. For his Senior Recital he presented a program composed entirely of his own works.

At Hampton he studied composition with R. Nathaniel Dett (see page 24), violin and arranging with Clarence Cameron White, and organ with Ernest Hays. He received his Bachelor of Science in Music from Hampton Institute in 1935. That same year he started his graduate work and took a post as director of music at the Dilliard High School in Goldsboro, North Carolina.

In 1936 he became Director of Music for the Palmer Memorial Institute in Sedalia, North Carolina. He became Director of Music at Teacher's College in Winston Salem, North Carolina in 1938 and remained in this post until 1941.

In 1941 he became Conductor of the Hampton Institute Choir and assistant to the head of the Music Department. He continued in these duties until 1944.

He served in the Navy during World War II from 1944 to 1947. While in the Navy he conducted a Navy Band stationed at Hampton Institute. He received the War Writer's prize for "A Sea Suite for Male Voices." Upon release from the Navy in 1947 he completed a Master of Music at the University of Michigan and took a post as Director of Music and Choir Director of the Norfolk Division of Virginia State College. Later that year he married Georgia Atkins. Dr. Georgia Atkins Ryder is a musician and is presently the chairman of the Music Department at Norfolk State College (Formerly known as the Norfolk Division of Virginia State College). He remained at the Norfolk Division of Virginia State College until 1962.

From his marriage to Georgia Atkins there is one son and two daughters: Olive Diana, Malcolm Elliot, and Aleta Renee. By an earlier marriage Mr. Ryder had one other son Victor Walker Ryder, who is a pianist. Victor W. Ryder was on the faculty at Fisk University and is now performing in Germany.

In 1948 Noah F. Ryder became a member of the American Society of Composers Authors and Publishers (ASCAP). Later that year he became Director of Music at the Banks Street Baptist Church in Norfolk, Virginia. He served at the Banks Street Baptist Church for 13 years. He also directed the Harry T. Burleigh Club of Hampton, Virginia. (See page 50.) He was also a member of the Federation of Male Glee Clubs of Virginia.

Mr. Ryder belonged to the American Guild of Organists, the American Federation of Musicians and the Music Educators National Conference. In 1948 he won an Omega Psi Phi grant for creative work and distinguished community service.
Noah Francis Ryder composed band, choral and piano music but he will best be remembered for his choral arrangement of "Let Us Break Bread Together." This piece has been one of the pillars of Afro-American Spirituals. One other very popular choral arrangement of his is "Gonna Journey Away" and it was through this piece that I first became acquainted with his work.

Two of his current publishers are: Handy Brothers Music Co, New York J. Fischer and Brother, Glen Rock, N.J.
(See Reflections page 138)

William Warfield

William Warfield
1921 – August 25, 1992
Bass-Baritone

William Warfield was born in West Helina, Arkansas. He grew up in Rochester, New York. His father Robert E. Warfield, was a Baptist Minister and his mother was a housewife. His father worked during the week collecting refuse. Mr. Warfield has five brothers.

As a young boy William Warfield sang soprano. By the time he reached high school his voice had deepened and had already begun to show a lot of promise. His music teacher entered him in the Music Educators National Conference competition, which he won. Upon graduation from high school he entered the Eastman School of Music of the University of Rochester, on a scholarship. He graduated from the Eastman School of Music with a Bachelor of Arts and began his Masters there. He was close to completing his Masters degree at Eastman when he received a chance to do some acting. He left school and went on the road with an acting company, which was performing "Call Me Mister." He later appeared in several other theatrical performances among them: "Set My People Free" and "Regina."

While at Eastman William Warfield did a lot of linguistic studies. Because of this knowledge of languages, upon his induction into the armed service, he was placed into the Secret Service. He speaks French, German and Italian fluently and also sings in Latin, Hungarian, Hebrew, Yiddish and Russian. While in the service he practiced constantly. One ex-G.I. who served with him said, "The man was always singing."

After he was released from the service, William Warfield continued his career and appeared in a production of "Porgy and Bess" in which he met and later married his leading lady whose name is Leontyne Price. They are now divorced.

In 1950 Mr. Warfield made his concert debut at Town Hall. Later that year he sang at the White House at the invitation of President Harry Truman. The occasion was a ceremony celebrating the 150th Anniversary of the moving of the Capital from Philadelphia to Washington D.C. And in that same season he appeared in the MGM film version of "Showboat." Between 1952 and 1959 William Warfield made five State Department concert tours covering 75,000 miles.

107

Mr. Warfield has concertized extensively in Europe extensively and has sung all over the world, including London, Iran, Pakistan, India, Canada, Australia and South America.

He is also well known for an unusually wide range.

He now holds an Honorary Doctorate of Laws Degree from the University of Arkansas. He is an Ellington Fellow at Yale University and presently a Professor of Music at the University of Illinois in Urbana, Illinois.

His discography includes:
----------   "Four Serious Songs" by Brahms
----------   "Porgy and Bess" by Gershwin
(RCA Victor)   "   "   "   (Excerpts)
----------   "The Messiah" by Handel (Leonard Bernstein, New York Philharmonic)
----------   "The Messiah" by Handel (Eugene Ormandy, Philadelphia Orchestra) (Columbia) "Requiem" by Mozart
"   "Old American Songs" ---Copeland
(MGM) "Showboat"
(Columbia)   "
(RCA Victor)   "

André Watts
Courtesy Ms. Alix B. Williamson, manager

Andre Watts
Born June 20, 1946 –
Pianist

Andre Watts was born in Nuremburg, Germany while his father, who was a Black soldier was stationed there. His mother, Maria Alexandra Watts was born in Hungary. His mother is also a pianist, as well as, a student of languages. Mr. Watts began to study the violin at the age of 4. By the time he was 6 it became evident to his parents that he preferred the piano. He received his first piano lessons from his mother. Later his family moved to Philadelphia. It was shortly after this that he began taking lessons at the Philadelphia Music Academy where he studied with Doris Bawden, Genia Robinor and Clement Petrillo. Mr. Watts attended a Catholic elementary school as well as a Quaker elementary School.

In 1955 at the age of 9 he competed against 40 other young gifted musicians for an engagement to play at the Philadelphia Orchestra's Children's Concerts. Mr. Watts won the competition and made his debut later that year at the Robin Hood Dell with the Philadelphia Orchestra.

In 1956 Andre Watts was invited back to the Robin Hood Dell to play the Mendelssohn "G Minor Piano Concerto" with the Philadelphia Orchestra.

When he was 14, Mr. Watts was brought back to the Philadelphia Academy of Music by the Philadelphia Orchestra to play the Symphonic Variations" by Cesar Franck.

In 1963 at the recommendation of his teachers he went to New York to audition for the Young People's Concerts of the New York Philharmonic. Miss Helen Coates, who was Maestro Bernstein's first piano teacher and now serves as Mr. Bernstein's secretary, sent for the Maestro immediately after hearing Mr. Watts. Maestro Bernstein, who was at that time the Conductor of the New York Philharmonic, was completely overwhelmed by Mr. Watts' playing and presented him that season. For his CBS Television Debut he played the Liszt "E Flat Piano Concerto." The composition was performed with such virtuosity that fan mail poured in from all over the country. The executives of CBS had never seen such a response to any other performance of Classical music. It was through this performance however that Andre Watts became the first Black instrumentalist in this Century to perform as a soloist with the New York Philharmonic.

According to recent research done by Professor Paul Giass of Brooklyn College it now appears that the first Black to perform as a soloist with the New York Philharmonic was the Black, Cuban born violinist Joseph White in 1875. However Mr. Watts was the first Black of American and Hungarian ancestry to play as a soloist with the New York Philharmonic.

Three weeks after his first appearance with the New York Philharmonic Glenn Gould was scheduled to do a performance with the New York Philharmonic. Mr. Gould became ill two days before the performance. He informed Leonard Bernstein that he would not be able to perform. The Maestro called Mr. Watts, who had returned to Philadelphia to continue his studies, and asked if he would return to play the Liszt Concerto with the Orchestra. Mr. Watts consented and this was the final piece of publicity that launched him on an important career.

The first year after his Philharmonic debut, his manager accepted only six concerts. His manager felt that a young artist must be given time to continue his studies and to grow.

Mr. Watts later attended the Peabody Conservatory in Baltimore, Maryland where he graduated with an Artist's diploma. At Peabody he studied piano with Leon Fleisher.

Between 1964 and 1966 he made appearances with a dozen major U.S. symphonic orchestras.

In 1966 he made his European debut with the London Symphony.

In 1967 he celebrated his 21st birthday by signing a long-term exclusive contract with CBS Records. Later that year he made a world tour for the U.S. State Department with the Los Angeles Philharmonic under the baton of Zubin Mehta. While on the State Department tour he made appearances in: Paris, Munich, Milan, Athens, Teheran, Iran, and many other cities throughout the world.

He celebrated the fifth anniversary of his New York Philharmonic debut with a return engagement in January 1969.

Since that return engagement, André Watts' concert schedule now averages 100 concerts a year and he is booked up three seasons in advance.

In the spring of 1973 on a two week U. S. State Department tour, he made his Russian debut as a soloist with the San Francisco Symphony.

Prior to leaving for Russia, Mr. Watts at 26 became the youngest person to receive an Honorary Doctorate of Music from Yale University in more than 200 years. The Honorary Doctorate and a citation were conferred upon him at Yale's 272nd Commencement by Dr. Kingsman Brewster, Jr.

When Pierre Boulez succeeded Mr. Bernstein as conductor of the New York Philharmonic, Andre Watts was the first soloist chosen by Maestro Boulez for his opening season.

In April 1973 the Philadelphia Orchestra invited him to join them in commemorating the 100th Anniversary of Rachmaninoff by playing the Third Rachmaninoff Piano Concerto.

On Lincoln Center's "Great Performers at Philharmonic Hall" series (now Avery Fischer Hall), he is the only artist to have been re-engaged eight years in succession and the only one to have sold out the huge auditorium each time.

He has been the subject of an hour-long NET Television special filmed during his preparation of a Mozart piano concerto with Zubin Mehta and the Los Angeles Philharmonic, as well as a CRS "Camera Three" show devoted to music of Franz Liszt, rarely heard, which he both played and discussed.

In Vienna he was asked to perform the great Brahms B-Flat Concerto in the Grosser Musikvereinsaal, where Brahms himself often conducted.

He has received numerous honors and awards in addition to the aforementioned.

He played at former President Nixon's Inaugural Concert at Constitution Hall in Washington, D. C.

He gave a concert in Teheran, Iran as part of the coronation festivities for the Shah of Iran. He ha also performed for the King and Queen of Greece.

President and Mrs. Mobuto of the Congo, upon hearing him at a State Dinner at the White House, presented him with the Congo's highest honor, the Order of Zaire.

Thus far he has mastered and performed more than 100 recital pieces from Haydn to Debussy and more than 20 concerts, including the rarely performed Rimsky-Korsakoff and MacDowell Concerti.

Mr. Watts still practices six hours a day, which is what has enabled him to continue his phenomenal growth.

In the rare moments that he has spare time, he reads Chekhov, Poe and Gibran; practices yoga for relaxation. He also listens to other keyboard masters, singers, and performers of the Flamenco Guitar School.

At present his discography is as follows:
Andre Watts on Columbia Records:
Beethoven: "Sonata in D Major", "Thirty two Variations", "Fur Elise","Rage Over a Lost Penny" M33074

Brahms: "Concerto No. 2 in B-Flat Major" (with Leonard Bernstein and the New York Philharmonic) MS 7134

113

Chopin: "Concerto No. 2 in F. Minor" (with Thomas Schippers and the New York Philharmonic) ML 6355/MS 6955

Franck: "Symphonic Variations" (with Erich Leinsdorf and the London Symphony Orchestra M33072 Also Liszt: "Todtentanz"

Liszt: "Concerto No.1 in E-Flat" (with Leonard Bernstein and New York Philharmonic   ML 6355/MS 6955

Liszt: "Sonata in B Minor" and "Six Paganini Etudes" M30488

Rachmaninoff: "Concerto No. 3 in D Major" (with Seiji Ozawa and the New York Philharmonic) M30059

Schubert: "Wanderer Fantasie, Op. 15", "Sonata in A Minor", "Waltzes, Op. 18" M33073

An Andre Watts Recital: Haydn: "Sonata No. 52 in E-Flat
Liszt: "Paganini Etude No. 2"
Chopin: "Nocturne, Op. 48, No. 1"
Debussy: "La Cathedrale Engloutie"
Liszt: "Sonnetto No. 104 del Patrarca" ML 6036/MS 6636

Watts Plays Chopin: "Sonata No. 2 in B-Flat Minor, Op. 35"
"Fantasie in F Minor, Op. 49"
"Etude in C. Major, Op. 10, No. 1"
"Etude in C-Sharp Minor, Op. 25, No. 7"
"Etude in C Minor, Op. 25, No. 12"
Tchaikovsky: "Concerto No. 1 in B-Flat" (with Leonard Bernstein and the New York Philharmonic) M33073

114

presents

INTERNATIONALLY ACCLAIMED

CAMILLA *Williams* Soprano

115

Camilla Williams
October 18, 1919 - January 29, 2012
Soprano, Teacher

Camilla Williams was born in Danville, Virginia. Her father and mother were Cornelius Booker Williams and Fanny Williams. Miss Williams was the youngest of four children; one of the three older offspring was a sister.

As a little girl of nine she was seen dancing very skillfully on her toes while playing. Her parents decided that they should start to encourage whatever talent she might have and placed her in an operetta. They felt that this was an indication of what was to come.

She attended Virginia State College, where she completed a Bachelor of Science degree with a major in music education in 1941. From 1941 to 1942 she taught in the town of Danville.

She attended the University of Pennsylvania for her graduate work. While in Pennsylvania she began to study privately with Madame Marion Szekely-Freschl.

In 1943 after only six months of study with Madame Szekely-Freschl she won the Marian Anderson Scholarship (see page 20).

In 1944 Camilla Williams signed a contract with RCA Records, won the Philadelphia Orchestra Youth Auditions and won the Marian Anderson Scholarship for a second time. The prize for the Philadelphia Orchestra Youth Auditions was a performance with the Orchestra.

She made her debut with the New York City Center Opera Company in 1946. This made her the first Black to sing Grand Opera with a professional American opera company. In singing the title role of "Madame Butterfly" with the New York City Center Opera Company, she became the first Black to sing this role with a major American opera company. This performance took place under the direction of Laszlo Halasz.

In 1948 she became the first Black to sing the title role of "Aida" with the New York City Center Opera Company.

116

In 1950 she took part in the first New York performance of Mozart's "Idomeneo." This performance was done with the Little Orchestra Society.

Between 1946 and 1951 she made 12 concert tours of Europe. At this point the State Department invited her to do a tour of 14 North and Central African countries. She was so well received that the State Department asked her to tour Ireland; Southeast Asia, to include Vietnam, Korea, Laos and Formosa; the Far East, Australia, and New Zealand.

In 1951 she signed a contract with Columbia Records.

She signed a contract with MGM Studios in 1952.

In 1955 she took part in the first Viennese performance of The Saint of Bleecker Street" by Menotti.

As the guest of President Eisenhower in 1960 she performed a concert for the Crown Prince of Japan.

In 1971 she took part in the first New York performance of "Orlando" by Handel and was listed in the first edition of "Who's Who in the World".

Miss Williams has concertized in every state in the Union except Hawaii. She was the first major artist to do a concert tour of Alaska before it gained statehood. She has concertized in Canada, South America; among the European countries, she has concertized in England, Germany, Switzerland, Austria and Italy. She has also toured Israel.

She has appeared with the Royal Philharmonic Orchestra, the Vienna Symphony, the BBC Orchestra, the Zurich Orchestra, the Geneva Symphony, the Berlin Philharmonic, the Belgium Symphony, the New York Philharmonic, the Chicago Symphony, and others.

She has received many honorary degrees and awards: including:
The Virginia State College 75th Anniversary Certificate
The Presidential Citation from New York University
She was honored as a "Distinguished Virginian" by Governor Linwood Holton of
Virginia

The Newspaper Guild Award as First Lady of American Opera
The Newspaper Guild "Page One Award"
The Chicago Defender's Honor Roll for bringing Democracy to Opera
A Gold Medal from the Emperor of Ethiopia
The Key to the Island of Taiwan (also known as Formosa) (The last two awards
were during a cultural exchange of President Johnson's administration)
The Art, Culture and Civic Guild Award for contributions to music presented by
Noble Sissle
The Negro Musicians Association Plaque
Harlem Opera and World Fellowship Society Award
WLI3 Radio Award for contributions to music
Listed in Danville, Virginia Museum of Fine Arts, the History Hall of Fame
Camilla Williams Park designated in Danville, Virginia

Her husband was the late Charles Beavers, a civil rights lawyer. They were happily married until his untimely death in the 1960's. This brought their marriage of 19 years to a close. In her own words, "He was a wonderful guy."

She has instructed at the Manhattan School of Music. She has taught at Brooklyn College, to which I can personally testify that she will be missed by all aspiring musicians.

She is presently teaching at Bronx Community College, Queens College, and privately. She also teaches at Talent Unlimited, at which Dr. John Motley, is Director (see page 108). It is marvelous that this artist takes time from a busy concert schedule to teach young people the art of singing with a good vocal technique.

Among the works she has recorded are:
Columbia: "Porgy and Bess" by Gershwin
MGM: "Highlights of Aida" by Verdi
"   "Spirituals"
"   "Art Songs"

John W. Work Jr.
Picture courtesy Mrs. John W. Work III

John Wesley Work, Junior
August 8, 1873 - September 8, 1926
Musicologist, Arranger

John Wesley Work, Junior was born in Nashville, Tennessee. His father, John Wesley Work, Senior, worked in a furniture store. His mother, Samuella Boyd Work was a housewife. There were several boys in his family but only two others, Frederick Jerome Work and Russell Work lived to adulthood. John W. Work Jr. also had three sisters: (I have included their married names) Jennie Work Ballentyne, Julia Work, and Elnora Work Shackleford Conn.

John W. Work Jr. attended the Pearl High School in Nashville. He then went on to Fisk University, which is also in Nashville, to do his undergraduate work. Upon completion of his undergraduate studies at Fisk, he began his graduate studies there and then went on to Harvard to complete them.

In 1898 upon completion of his graduate studies at Harvard he returned to Fisk University and became Professor of Latin and Greek in addition to conductor of the Choir and the Fisk Jubilee Singers. He developed the Fisk Jubilee Singers to such a level of professionalism that they became the first Black group to record for RCA Victor Records. He taught at Fisk for 25 years. There he met and married Agnes Morris Haynes who was one of the Fisk Jubilee Singers. To this marriage were born: John W. III, Merrill C., Julian C., and two girls, Helen E. and Frances Work Alston (married name).

In 1923 he was elected President of Roger Williams University, which was also in Nashville. He resigned his post at Fisk and went to Roger Williams University where he remained the rest of his career.

He collected many spirituals and published a book of spirituals entitled "Folk Songs of The American Negro." He is responsible for the documentation of many Afro-American Spirituals.

One of his sons, John Wesley Work III was also a musician. He achieved even greater fame as a musician than his father. We will discuss him next. (See next sketch.)

Dr. John W. Work III
Picture courtesy Mrs. John W. Work III

John Wesley Work III
June 15,1901 - May 19,1967
Arranger, Composer, Conductor

John W. Work III was born in Tullahoma, Tennessee. His father John W. Work, Jr. (see previous sketch) was a musician and a college instructor. His mother, Agnes Morris Haynes Work was a former Fisk Jubilee Singer and a housewife. He had two brothers and two sisters. (See previous sketch.)

He attended the Fisk University Training School, for grammar school.. He then attended Fisk University High School and its college level. While in high school he began to compose. In 1923 he received his Bachelor of Arts degree from Fisk University. After graduation he went to the Institute of Musical Studies, which was later absorbed by the Juilliard School of Music. He attended the Institute of Musical Studies for a year and a half. Upon the death of his parents, he returned to Fisk University and took over the Men's Glee Club. He conducted the Men's Glee Club from 1927 to 1931. He then went to Columbia University in New York where he earned a Master of Arts degree and received a Julius Rosenwald Scholarship, which enabled him to earn a Bachelor of Music Degree at Yale.

He later became Professor of Theory and Chairman of the Music Department at Fisk.

In 1946 he won first prize in a competition of the Fellowship of American Composers for "The Singers" written for chorus and orchestra.

In 1948 he began to conduct the Fisk Jubilee Singers and continued to do so until 1957. In 1965 he retired from his position as chairman of the Music Department for health reasons. He continued to teach Theory at Fisk until 1966.

In 1967 Dr. Work passed away. At the time of his death he was survived by his wife, Mrs. Edith McFall Work, two sons John Wesley Work IV and Frederick Taylor Work and seven grandchildren among them John W. Work V.

Dr. John W. Work III has written a book entitled "American Negro Songs."

Dr. Work was also a member of the American Society of Composers Authors and Publishers (ASCAP).

122

Most Black Church choirs have sung "Rockin' Jerusalem" which was arranged by John Work III. I believe he will always be remembered for this arrangement. One other arrangement of his that will help to make him immortal is "Lord I'm Out Here On Your Word" for tenor solo and chorus. A complete listing of his arrangements and original compositions including published and unpublished works includes over 100 compositions. A partial listing of some of his other popular works is as follows:

1. "This Little Light O' Mine "Publisher, Galaxy Music Corp., New York (Soprano and Chorus)
2. "Done Made My Vow To The Lord " " (Tenor and Chorus)
3. "Is A Light Shining In The Heavens Publisher, Hanse Publishing Co. (soprano and chorus)
4. "New Born" Pub. J. Fischer and Bro. A Division of Belwin Mills Publishing Co., Melville, New York
5. "Rise Up Shepherd and Foller" Broadman Press (Chorus)

Music Building, **Norfolk State College** (1970)

Reflections
Norfolk State College

The Music Department of Norfolk State College had a modest beginning. In 1947 when Noah Francis Ryder went to the Norfolk Division of Virginia Union University (now Norfolk State College) to become a member of its faculty he was the only person in the music department.

In 1947 Georgia Atkins came to the Norfolk Division of Virginia Union University as a student. She became the accompanist for the choir. Upon her graduation she joined the music faculty at the Norfolk Division of Virginia Union University. For a while they were the only members of the music faculty there. Noah Francis Ryder and Georgia Atkins were later married.

From 1947 to 1955 N.F. Ryder taught at the Norfolk Division of Virginia Union University while it was located on Fenchurch Street. There is only one building on Fenchurch Street. But to my knowledge the college no longer uses this building.

From 1955 to 1962 he taught at what is now known as Brown Hall, which is located on the present campus site. He died before the music department moved into its present building. On February 1,1969, the Norfolk Division of Virginia Union University was given permission to become an independent college and its name was changed to Norfolk State College. In 1970 the Music Department moved into its present building. (See Picture.)

Dr. Georgia Atkins Ryder is presently the head of the Music Department at Norfolk State College. The music Department now numbers 24.

The present building has six floors containing numerous practice rooms, lecture rooms and separate rooms for the band and chorus.

The campus is in a beautiful area located near the central section of the city of Norfolk with over a half dozen different buildings. There are many large well-kept lawns, which are beautiful to the eye and inspiring to the mind.

I felt truly inspired as I spoke to Dr. G.A. Ryder. She is a fountain of knowledge on various Black musicians and the history of Norfolk College.

125

Music Building, **Hampton Institute** (1970)

Reflections
Hampton Institute

The present music building at Hampton Institute (see picture) is named for the founder of the Institute, General Samuel Chapman Armstrong. There is a plaque located on the first floor dedicated to R. Nathaniel Dett and the work he did there. The Armstrong Building (Music Building) is located near the main entrance of the campus.

The room where the chorus and band rehearses is well constructed. It has a semi-circular shape with step-like levels going from the actual floor of the room, where the conductor would be located to the highest level of the room, where the doors are located. Most importantly, the room allows each instrumentalist or singer an ideal view of the conductor.

GLOSSARY

Alto - There are several schools of thought about this voice range. Some musicians feel that these singers are merely sopranos who have a very weak upper range and therefore are better suited to this medium voice part. Other conductors feel that this is actually a medium voice range and a separate entity unto itself, depending upon the time period it was sometimes used as a shortened form of the word contralto. (See below.)

Baritone- The medium mature male voice.

Bass - The lowest mature male voice. In actuality the lowest of all voices. (There are several type of basses but for our purposes we do not need quite so fine a distinction.)

Bass-Baritone - A baritone with a very dark quality to his voice and a more than average lower range to his voice These baritones are able to sing some of the higher Bass roles.

Contralto - The lowest of all the treble voices. Some musicians feel that the contralto and the Mezzo-Soprano are actually the same voice range. In actuality they are not. The contralto usually has a better lower register and can sing low notes that the mezzo-soprano is not capable of reaching. Some contraltos have been known to extend their upper range and sing some of the mezzo roles but there is a difference in the sound. These are usually exceptional contraltos. I would venture to say that the average contralto usually cannot reach the high notes of the mezzo range.

Counter-Tenor - A man who continues to sing a treble voice naturally past age 13, whose voice has never changed to one of the mature male voices. A true counter-tenor for the most part cannot sing a mature male voice part. (See below.)

Falsetto - This is the art of a man singing with the remnants of the treble voice he used as a small boy. The man who has a good falsetto can be used in place of a counter-tenor but these men can, at will sing a mature male voice part.

Librettist - a more elaborate term for a lyricist (See below), however a librettist is usually more involved with writing the words for an opera. Lyricist - A person who writes words for vocal music.

Lyric Soprano - These are the highest and lightest sopranos. (There are two main types of lyric sopranos.)

Lyric Spinto Soprano - These are sopranos who have the same range as a lyric soprano but their quality is a little heavier than the lyric sopranos.

Mature Male Voices - Voices sung by boys 13 and older and men, specifically: Tenor, Baritone and Bass. These voices are sometimes called male voices. This is misleading because it does not take into consideration the fact that young boys sing treble parts.

Mezzo-Soprano - These are the lowest of all the sopranos and have a very heavy quality to their voices. Many conductors use them to sing with the altos (see above) on choral massages. They are sometimes used to sing contralto solos (see above) where the solo does not go below the end of the Mezzo range.

Mixed Voices - Any vocal ensemble or piece of music, that uses some combination of treble and mature male voices.

Musicologist - A historian who specializes in the study of music history; these are usually musicians who devote some of their time to the study of music history.

Prosthetics - The study of artificial limbs.

Scenario - Webster defines scenario as an outline or synopsis of a play

Soprano - The highest treble voice. There are various types of sopranos. Some of these classifications refer to range while others refer to differences in quality (see above)

Treble voices - Voices sung by women, girls and boy younger than 13. Specifically: soprano alto, and contralto (see above)

Vocal Music - Music for the voice

INDEX

130

BIBLIOGRAPHY

Allen, Sanford - Publicity Release
Amsterdam News - Various dates
Anderson,Marian - My Lord What A Morning Viking Press N'.Y.,N.Y. 1972

ASCAP Biographical Directory
Christian –Century
Concise Dictionary of Singers
Cuney-Hare,Maude - Negro Musicians and Their Music Da Capo Press, N.Y.C. 1974

Current Biography
Daily News - May 3, 1973 and other dates
Daily Worker
De Lerma, Dominique-Rene - Introduction to the Collected Piano Works of R. Nathaniel Dett Summy-Birchard, Evanston, Illinois 1973

DePaur, Leonard - Personal Vitae
Dispeker, Thea - Publicity Release on Martina Arroyo
Ebony -December 1951 and other dates
Greensboro Daily Helm,McKinley - Angel Mot and Her Son Roland
Hayes Little, Brown and Company, Boston 1942

Herald Tribune - various dates Johnson, James Weldon - Along This Way, Viking Press N.Y.C. 1961
Lovingood,Penman - Famous Modern Negro Musicians Press Forum Company Brooklyn, N.Y. 1921

Music Standard - London Newspaper, January to June 1920
Newsweek - February 11,1963 and other dates
New York Post - August 19,1970 and other dates
New York Times - various dates
Opera News - various dates
Roach, Hildred - Black American Music Past and Present Crescendo Publishing Company, Boston 1973
Robeson, Paul - Here I Stand, Beacon Press, Boston 1972
Ryder, Georgia A. - Biographical Sketch on Noah Francis Ryder
Schomburg Collection - New York Public Library, N.Y.C. Various reports
Virginia Pilot - (Newspaper), Norfolk, Virginia Who's Who in America - 1972,1973
146

www.ingramcontent.com/pod-product-compliance
Lightning Source LLC
Chambersburg PA
CBHW060806050426
42449CB00008B/1566